Youth Ministry in Africa

HIPPOBOOKS

This book is written with Africa in mind. It helps to give African youth an identity by offering a fission from Western expressions of spirituality, sexuality, and youth culture. Forging an African identity is critical to empowering youth participation within their worshipping community and society at large. In this day and age, where conspiracy theories and suspect philosophies rule the internet space, forging a Christian identity as a youth in Africa is critical. It aids in understanding God's world around them and helps to build capacity to seize opportunities for participation in church and society. This book is an eye-opener for all who interact with young people in institutions of learning, church, and family. It enables all participants to intentionally make way for the youth to become who God has called them to be.

Rev. Mukomunene Muthuri, DMin
Youth and Teens Minister,
Lavington United Church, Nairobi, Kenya

As a youth pastor, it can sometimes be challenging to locate books that reflect the evolving nature of African youth, youth ministry, and the influence of surrounding culture. This book not only captures these aspects but also provides a path forward.

Kwizera Samuel
Youth Pastor, New Life Bible Church, Rwanda

This book brings together much-needed responses to significant questions facing African society concerning youth and how to minister to them. There has been a long overdue need for books on youth ministry within the African context to help build a counter-movement against the onslaught of neo-colonial, foreign, and ungodly concepts and lifestyles being peddled as human freedom. This book addresses pressing questions that must be answered in youth ministry today. Specifically, the deconstruction and reconstruction of thought and ethos in the light of the technological and ideological currents on the continent. Many young people are getting confused by the numerous efforts to remove godly reality from their daily lives. As a result, youth feel left out because they see the church and God as irrelevant. This is a storm that requires a lot of courage to stay its concomitant tide.

This book boldly contributes to the hard debates concerning youth on the African continent, covering topics such as sexuality and identity, spirituality, the biblical view of gender, and the role of the church in shaping the youth for Africa's development. I recommend this timely book which brings well-researched precision to the issues raised in the chapters. It is a must-read for all who desire to understand youth ministry from an African perspective.

Rev. Smith F. K. Tettey, PhD
Chairperson, Kumasi Presbytery, Global Evangelical Church
Research Associate, University of Pretoria, South Africa

Youth Ministry in Africa

A Biblical Perspective

Edited by
Nathan H. Chiroma

HIPPOBOOKS

© 2025 Nathan H. Chiroma

Published 2025 by HippoBooks
An imprint of Langham Publishing
www.langhampublishing.org

Langham Publishing and its imprints are a ministry of Langham Partnership

Langham Partnership
PO Box 296, Carlisle, Cumbria, CA3 9WZ, UK
www.langham.org

ISBNs:
978-1-83973-258-4 Print
978-1-78641-198-3 ePub
978-1-78641-231-7 PDF

British Library Cataloguing-in-Publication Data
A catalogue record for this book is available from the British Library

ISBN: 978-1-83973-258-4

Cover & Book Design: projectluz.com

Contents

Foreword

Africa is a youthful continent. But youthfulness, if left untended, either erupts into a raging wildfire – or fades into wasted potential. Yet under the care of thoughtful shepherds, youthfulness is a blessing to light pathways, warm communities, and drive transformation. That is what youth ministry must do – and that is precisely what *Youth Ministry in Africa* offers.

This book is more than a collection of papers. It is a bold theological statement, crafted by some of Africa's most renowned scholars and seasoned practitioners in youth ministry. These contributors are not armchair theorists – they are theologians of the street, the campus, the pulpit, and the prayer room. Each chapter pulses with both academic rigor and pastoral heartbeat, speaking directly into the lives, struggles, and aspirations of African youth.

At the helm of this important work is Dr. Nathan H. Chiroma – a mentor to youth ministry scholars, a pastor to pastors, and a prophetic voice in African theological circles. Nathan does not merely write about young people – he walks with them. His deep faith in their potential, his commitment to placing them at the center of the church's life, and his lived experience across diverse African contexts make him one of the continent's most trusted guides in this space. For me, he is both a colleague and a mentor – one whose vision has shaped many of us who serve the next generation.

The chapters in this book engage urgent and contemporary issues: from sexual orientation and identity to spirituality, digital culture, social justice, and transformative development. These are not abstract concerns; they are the actual questions young Africans are asking. The book offers a theological and pastoral compass for churches, youth workers, and communities trying to find their bearing in these rapidly shifting landscapes.

But more than responding to issues, this book raises a timely challenge: How does the church become a thought leader? Too often theology in Africa has taken the position of a late responder – arriving at the scene after culture has already drawn conclusions. This book urges the church to be prophetically proactive, thinking and acting ahead of crises, not behind them. It challenges us to move beyond theological corners – where we whisper among ourselves – and step boldly into the public square, shoulder to shoulder with educators, economists, psychologists, artists, scientists, and civic leaders. Only through collaboration across disciplines can we envision and deliver what this continent desperately needs: an abundant community where young people thrive spiritually, socially, and structurally.

For what is the end of theologizing if not faithful presence and prophetic action? Theology is not complete when a doctrine is clarified – it is complete when lives are transformed. When rightly done, theology does not end in libraries but in real lives – in classrooms and slums, in youth fellowships and online forums, where young Africans search for meaning, hope, and truth.

That is what this book offers. It gives us not only ideas but a vision – a vision of youth ministry as a response to Africa's greatest opportunity: its young people. It frames youth not as passive receivers of care but as participants in God's mission. It invites the church to stop underestimating youth and start unleashing them.

To read *Youth Ministry in Africa* is to encounter both clarity and conviction. It is to remember that youth ministry is not a footnote in ecclesiology – it is a front line in missiology. Whether you are a student, a pastor, a policymaker, or a concerned parent – this book will challenge you, equip you, and stir you toward action.

May you read with open eyes and an expectant heart – for the future of the church in Africa depends on how we see, engage, and invest in its youth.

Edward Buri
Presbyterian Minister and Youth Champion,
Nairobi, Kenya

Introduction

Africa's population includes a growing proportion of young people. Adolescents possess abundant energy that should be channelled towards constructive endeavours. As of 2015, global data from the United Nations indicated that there were around 1.2 billion individuals between the ages of twelve and twenty-four, representing 17 percent of the global population. This number is projected to rise to 1.3 billion by the year 2030. Africa is particularly affected by this global trend due to its high population of young people. In 2015, the UN reported that Africa had a population of 226 million young people between the ages of fifteen and twenty-four, which accounted for almost 20 percent of the continent's total population and one-fifth of the global youth population. If individuals under the age of thirty-five are also to be considered, then young people make up an astonishing 75 percent of the total population of Africa. Furthermore, by 2030, it is projected that Africa's youth will account for 42 percent of the global youth population, and this proportion is likely to keep rising, more than doubling by 2055.

Bience Philomena Gawanas, the Special Adviser on Africa to the United Nations from 2018 to 2020, highlighted that Africa has the highest proportion of young people in the world. Approximately 220 million individuals, which accounts for 20 percent of the continent's population, are between the ages of fifteen and twenty-four. To fully capitalize on this demographic dividend, Gawanas emphasized the need to take immediate action to address challenges to peace and security, such as radicalization, violent extremism, sexual violence, xenophobia, and forced migration. She cautioned against implementing oppressive laws based on inaccurate generalizations and highlighted the African Union's Agenda 2063 and its comprehensive plan to achieve peace by 2020, urging increased assistance from the United Nations, regional organizations, and the private sector.

The growing youth population presents both opportunities and challenges. Numerous individuals in the corporate sector have capitalized on this demographic trend to advance their economic goals by actively involving young people. The key question is how the church is utilizing the youth population in Africa to its advantage. In many churches, young people are frequently viewed with suspicion, being perceived as potential threats rather than as valuable assets and as challenges that need to be resolved rather than opportunities that should be nurtured. This book aims to provide parents, youth workers, churches, and Christian communities with the necessary tools to engage with young people in a meaningful and theologically sound manner, addressing issues that impact their overall development. While there are numerous theological books on youth ministry, these books often approach the subject from a Western perspective. This book seeks to fill that gap by offering guidance that is relevant and applicable to a wider audience.

The initial chapter addresses the highly relevant matter of sexual orientation among adolescents. Many young people experience confusion due to the multitude of theories and ideologies surrounding sex and sexuality. Thus, this chapter presents a biblical framework that will assist young people, parents, and youth workers to effectively navigate this complex and delicate subject. The second chapter provided an in-depth exploration of the relationship between young people and culture. Youth are part of a rapidly changing culture, and they often face challenges in understanding and navigating it. This chapter presents a cogent thesis on how parents and youth workers can comprehend the culture of young people, while also explaining how young people can establish connections with their own culture. The third chapter focuses on a fundamental tenet of youth and spirituality in Africa. Adolescents have a strong natural inclination towards spirituality. However, our comprehension of their spirituality presents an opportunity for meaningful engagement that can enrich their spiritual experiences. The fourth chapter explores the topics of youth and community development, emphasizing the significance of young people's participation in community development. Their engagement provides a pathway for their spiritual maturation and advancement. The fifth chapter emphasizes the importance of youth and transformative development. This chapter also presents a plan for practical implementation that promotes personal growth. The sixth chapter explains the process of establishing a digital milieu on social media platforms, which serves as platforms for the development of self-identity and the shaping of young people. The final chapter, titled "Youth and Social Justice," explores the contribution of young people in promoting fairness and equality, arguing that youth can be key advocates for justice within their diverse communities.

It is the significance of youth ministry in Africa, heightened by several continent-specific factors, that gave rise to the writing of this book for the following purposes:

1. Developing the next generation of influential leaders
    Africa possesses a demographically young population. Investing in
    youth ministry is essential for fostering and cultivating the future
    leaders for the continent.

2. Tackling societal issues
    Youth ministry is crucial in tackling the socio-economic difficulties
    faced by African youth, including unemployment, poverty, limited
    access to education, and health concerns. It offers direction and
    support in addressing these obstacles.

3. Growth in one's spiritual journey
    Youth ministry plays a crucial role in fostering the spiritual growth
    and development of young people. It establishes a solid foundation
    of moral and ethical principles that, in turn, have a beneficial influ-
    ence on their communities and the entire continent.

4. Involvement of the community
    Youth ministry mobilizes young individuals to actively participate
    in community development initiatives, fostering a sense of respon-
    sibility and ownership in tackling local challenges.

5. Promoting harmony and tranquillity
    Youth ministry has the potential to promote unity, reconciliation,
    and peacebuilding among young people in areas affected by conflict
    and social tensions. This can have a positive impact on the stability
    and harmony of African societies.

6. Enhancing autonomy and fostering the acquisition of new skills
    Youth ministry can empower young people by providing them with
    opportunities to enhance their skills, participate in mentorship
    programmes, and receive vocational training. This enables them
    to contribute meaningfully to the development and growth of their
    communities and continent.

7. Safeguarding cultural heritage
    Youth ministry may play a crucial role in safeguarding and advanc-
    ing African cultural values, customs, and traditions by fostering a
    strong sense of pride and identity among young people while adapt-
    ing to the evolving global environment.

Ultimately, youth ministry in Africa plays a crucial role in moulding the future of the continent by tackling social issues, developing leaders, promoting spiritual growth, and encouraging young people to make positive contributions to their communities and to society at large.

1

Youth and Sexuality

Obed L. Yusuf

Introduction

Sexuality is undoubtedly a fundamental part of human existence. Alongside fundamental needs like sleeping and eating, sexuality is a primary drive that is intricately woven into the fabric of human existence. Irrespective of who we are, every individual – young or old, male or female, African or American – is inherently a sexual being.[1] This means that human sexuality, contrary to popular opinion, is not an issue that is peculiar to young people or to young people in Africa. Rather, sexuality is an issue that affects every human being. As Kok emphasized, sexuality is not something that begins at puberty and disappears or fades away with age. Rather, sexuality is a vital part of human life, beginning well before birth and continuing throughout a person's life.[2]

While sexuality is intrinsic to human existence and not limited to young people, it is essential to note that navigating sexuality and related issues is particularly difficult for young people. This is because young people encounter diverse and sometimes conflicting messages about sexuality from the media, their peers, and educational institutions. Unfortunately, the church's voice is often faint or scarcely heard in the discourse on sexuality. One only needs to ask a group of young people where they learn about sexuality to discover that the top voices that speak to them about sexuality are social media, peers, the internet, and school. Seldom do young people learn about sexuality from the church or youth ministry. In the rare instances where young people do learn about sexuality from the church or in youth ministry, the message is often

---

1. DeLamater and Friedrich, "Human Sexual Development," 10.
2. Kok, "Sexuality," 39.

limited to teachings about sexual intercourse, where the central focus is on abstaining from any sexual activity until marriage.

One reason the church's voice is faint in addressing matters of youth and sexuality, especially in the African context, is the scarcity of resources that explore sexuality from a biblical and theological perspective. The lack of resources that address youth and sexuality from a biblical and theological standpoint in the African context has led many churches to develop a narrow view of sexuality. In Kenya, for example, most churches focus narrowly on specific aspects of sexuality, such as LGBTQAI+ issues. In addition, some churches have spiritualized sexuality by associating it with demonic expressions and depicting it as a matter that requires prayer and deliverance. This is often evident in the comments made, sermons preached, and prayers said from the pulpit against the spirit of homosexuality in some Kenyan churches.

Against this backdrop, this chapter is intended to assist the church and, by extension, the youth ministry in Africa to broaden their perspective on youth and sexuality and approach it in a more nuanced and informed manner. To accomplish this aim, the chapter begins by defining sexuality. After laying the foundation for the discussion by presenting a biblically informed definition of sexuality, the chapter evaluates the messages received by young people on sexuality in contemporary society. To equip churches and youth ministries in Africa to engage with these messages, it then outlines a biblical view of sexuality. The chapter then uses its biblically informed definition and depiction of sexuality to develop a theology of youth and sexuality, thereby offering a theological resource that helps churches and youth ministries in Africa to thoughtfully and compassionately engage with young people on this topic of sexuality. Utilizing its theology of youth and sexuality, the chapter then draws on the teachings of the apostle Paul to outline a model for engaging with this topic of youth and sexuality in Africa.

Sexuality Defined

Sexuality is a complex and multifaceted concept that is difficult to define accurately and concisely because of its inherent intricacy and multidimensional nature that draws on many disciplines.[3] This difficulty is not just a theoretical challenge for scholars from other disciplines. After reviewing the definitions of sexuality by various theologians, Closson concludes that the presence of multiple competing definitions of sexuality indicates a lack of consensus even

---

3. Kok, 39.

within the church and its theologians.[4] He goes on to state that this lack of consensus among theologians on defining sexuality is because of the absence of a textbook definition of sexuality in the Bible. Similarly, Magnuson observes that while the Bible portrays human beings as embodied creatures who are male and female and speaks unambiguously about sexual desire and sex, it does not explicitly define the concept of sexuality.[5]

Closson argues that while the Bible does not define sexuality, it does provide a robust framework for understanding it.[6] After describing this biblical framework, Magnuson offers this helpful definition in his *Invitation to Christian Ethics*:

> The Biblical [framework] suggests that human sexuality is a central aspect of who we are as human beings, which produces sexual desire, drawing us towards the one-flesh union of one man and one woman in marriage. [Therefore, based on this framework] sexuality is a way of describing the dynamic of maleness and femaleness, which produces a desire that moves male and female to be completed through an intimate bond that Genesis describes as a one-flesh union (Gen 2:24).[7]

Based on this biblical framework and definition, this chapter defines sexuality as the innate sexual feelings inherent in males and females and the expression of sexual desires for sexual intimacy with persons of the opposite sex. By "opposite sex," this chapter refers to relationships between male (man) and female (woman).[8] For a better understanding, I will break down this definition and explain the meaning of each phrase.

---

4. Closson, *Biblical Principles*, 7.

5. Magnuson, *Invitation to Christian Ethics*, 159.

6. Closson, *Biblical Principles*, 8.

7. Magnuson, *Invitation to Christian Ethics*, 159–60.

8. This chapter acknowledges that while various scholars draw distinctions between sex and gender, others still use the terms interchangeably (See Muehlenhard and Peterson, "Distinguishing between Sex and Gender," 791–803). Along with Muehlenhard and Peterson's conclusion (p. 801), this chapter affirms that the distinction between sex and gender will be less meaningful and less important over time. Thus, in keeping with the biblical framework for understanding sexuality, the chapter uses the term "sex" interchangeably with "gender" to refer to male (man) and female (woman).

Innate Sexual Feelings

The phrase "innate sexual feelings" refers to the natural, innate emotions and attractions that individuals experience. These feelings are not learned or acquired through external influences but are intrinsic to human biology. In other words, these innate sexual feelings are driven by biological processes – including genetics, hormones, and neurological factors – that work together to shape an individual's sexual attraction and drive. However, these biological processes do not create sexual feelings but only work to sustain their existence and development.

Inherent in Males and Females

The phrase "inherent in males and females" in this definition of sexuality refers to the biblical reality that innate sexual feelings are a universal human characteristic in all individuals. Both males and females possess these inherent sexual feelings as part of their natural make-up.

The Expression of Sexual Desires

The phrase "expression of sexual desires" refers to how males and females outwardly demonstrate or act upon their innate sexual feelings. This includes a wide range of behaviours, actions, and communications that convey sexual attraction and needs. In speaking of a wide range of behaviours, actions, and communications, I mean that (1) the expression of sexual desires can take many forms, such as physical gestures (for example, touching, kissing), verbal communication (for example, expressing attraction or love), and non-verbal cues (for example, body language, eye contact); (2) expressing sexual desires, while including physical actions, also involves emotional intimacy and building connection and affection between males and females; and (3) the expression of sexual desires requires clear and respectful communication, which includes discussing boundaries, consent, and mutual interests with one's partner to ensure that both males and females feel comfortable and valued. It is important to note that since different cultures have varying attitudes towards sexual behaviours, actions and communications, cultural norms and social expectations significantly influence how sexual desires are expressed.

For Sexual Intimacy

The phrase "for sexual intimacy" refers to close physical interactions driven by sexual attraction, such as kissing, hugging, caressing, and sexual intercourse. Sexual intimacy is a key aspect of sexuality, contributing to bonding and emotional closeness between a man and a woman. According to the proposed definition, which is informed by the biblical framework for understanding sexuality, sexual intimacy is to be experienced and expressed only within the context of marriage.

With Persons of the Opposite Sex

This phrase "with persons of the opposite sex" specifies that the innate sexual feelings inherent in males and females and the expression of sexual desires for sexual intimacy are to be directed towards persons of the opposite sex. This emphasizes heterosexual relationships, where men and women express sexual desires and seek sexual intimacy with the opposite sex – man to woman and woman to man.

Youth and Sexuality Conceptualized

In line with the biblically informed definition, youth and sexuality can be understood as the innate sexual feelings inherent in young people and their expression of sexual desires for sexual intimacy within the context of marriage with persons of the opposite sex. This implies that while sexuality is inherent in every human being, regardless of age, its expression should only be within the context of marriage. In other words, young people must understand that sexuality is fully expressed and experienced within the context of marriage. This is because the Bible clearly teaches that sexual intimacy is meant to be experienced within the context of marriage and that engaging in such intimacy outside marriage is a sin (Matt 5:28; 1 Cor 6:18; 7:1–2; 1 Thess 4:3). Therefore, young people must control their innate sexual feelings and refrain from expressing their sexual desires for sexual intimacy until they are married to someone of the opposite sex.

Sexuality through the Lens of the World

Sexuality, as a fundamental aspect of human existence, is often interpreted through various lenses. This is because sexuality encompasses biological, psychological, social, cultural, and individual dimensions that interact in unique ways. In Africa, the voice of the church and youth ministry has been faint in the discourse on sexuality, due largely to a lack of theological resources that can guide and inform their engagement. As a result, many young people have taken their cues on sexuality from the media, academic studies, marketing campaigns, and cultural norms. If the African church and youth ministry are to engage meaningfully with young people on the topic of sexuality, it is essential to examine the various messages – propagated through media, education, marketing campaigns, and cultural discourse – that inform and shape their perceptions and attitudes towards sexuality. To help the church in this task, this next section critically examines some key messages in contemporary society that inform and shape young people's perceptions and understanding of sexuality in Africa.

Sexuality as a Social Construct

One of the compelling messages in contemporary discourse that informs and shapes young people's perceptions and understanding of sexuality in Africa is the theory that sexuality is a social construct. This theory suggests that sexuality is not innate but is shaped by society. According to this approach, the roles associated with sexuality are assigned by society, often starting at birth when a doctor assigns sex based on physical characteristics. Butler, a prominent theorist in this field, challenges the notion that sexuality is innate.[9] She asserts that sexuality and sexual identities are constructed through social interactions and are subject to change over time, highlighting the fluidity and variability of human sexuality.

The idea that sexuality is a social construct emerges from the broader framework of social constructionism, a theory in sociology and anthropology that suggests that much of what we perceive as reality is shaped by social interactions. Early sociologists such as Durkheim and later theorists like Berger and Luckmann argue that knowledge and reality are products of social processes.[10] Based on this perspective, Foucault challenges the notion of sexuality as an innate phenomenon, arguing that it is deeply entwined with social institutions and heavily influenced by social context.[11] This implies that sexuality is malleable and subject to change over time and across different societies, as

---

9. Butler, *Gender Trouble*, 10–12.

10. Durkheim, "Elementary Forms," 52–67; see also Berger and Luckmann, "Social Construction of Reality," 110–22.

11. Foucault, *History of Sexuality*, 105–6.

opposed to this chapter's biblically informed definition that views sexuality as innate and unchanging.

This understanding of sexuality as a social construct profoundly shapes young people's perceptions in Africa, encouraging them to view sexuality as a spectrum with many possibilities. Through music, movies, marketing campaigns, educational settings, social media, and other influential platforms, young people in Africa are influenced by messages suggesting that sexuality is nuanced and flexible. This view also encourages young people in Africa to "break free" from the constraints of the "rigid" biblical definition that views sexuality as innate and unchanging and to perceive it as a spectrum that allows for fluidity and diversity.

Sexuality as a Choice

Contemporary discussions about sexuality also emphasize a narrative that champions personal autonomy in defining one's sexuality. At the core of this message is the idea that people have the right to make decisions about their sexuality without external coercion from societal or religious expectations. This narrative not only advocates for a person's freedom to choose their sexual partners, practices, and reproductive outcomes but also underscores personal autonomy as a powerful tool to resist social and religious norms that view sexuality as innate and unchanging.

By depicting sexuality as a choice, this narrative has negatively influenced young people in Africa to perceive and understand sexuality as something they can control and define based on personal experiences and desires. For example, in the 2017 Women's March Lusaka, protestors took to the streets, advocating for women's empowerment with slogans such as "My body, my sexuality. My right, my choice."[12] While the women protesting were advocating for gender equality and women's reproductive health rights, this slogan encapsulates the viewpoint that consent, freedom, and self-determination are crucial in matters of sexuality. It also suggests that decisions about sexuality are a matter of personal choice that should not be influenced or determined by external forces such as government policy, cultural norms, or religion.

---

12. Mogoatlhe, "Women in Zambia's Capital," https://www.globalcitizen.org/en/content/womens-march-movement-lusaka-2020/.

Sexuality as Identity

The final contemporary message about sexuality considered in this chapter is the idea that sexuality is a fundamental aspect of personal identity. This perspective suggests that a person's sexuality is central to their sense of self and plays a crucial role in how they understand and define themselves. This perspective emphasizes that sexuality is not just a physical or emotional experience but a core aspect of an individual's identity. Commenting on this perspective, Diamond states that this personal self-conception involves recognizing and embracing one's sexuality as a fundamental component of one's identity.[13]

This message has misled young people in Africa, leading them to believe that their sexuality is inseparable from their identity. For example, the increasing visibility of LGBTQAI+ characters and themes in films, television shows, and online content has contributed to normalizing and reinforcing the idea that sexuality is an essential part of a person's identity. Additionally, Amnesty International has revealed that social media platforms have become powerful tools for providing validation and solidarity to young people in Africa, reinforcing this understanding that their sexuality is a crucial aspect of who they are.[14]

Sexuality through the Lens of the Word

As noted earlier, this chapter aims to present a biblically informed definition of sexuality, evaluate the various contemporary messages in society that inform and shape young people's perception and understanding of sexuality in Africa, provide a biblical perspective on the discourse on sexuality, and develop a theology of youth and sexuality. The previous sections of this chapter defined sexuality from a biblical perspective as the innate sexual feelings inherent in males and females and the expression of sexual desires for sexual intimacy with persons of the opposite sex. In addition, the previous sections evaluated the contemporary messages in society that inform and shape young people's perception and understanding of sexuality in Africa: sexuality as a social construct, sexuality as a choice, and sexuality as a fundamental aspect of identity.

This section will explore how the Bible depicts sexuality. The discussion – based on critical analysis of the biblical narrative – will focus on how biblical characters outwardly express or act upon their innate sexual feelings and desire for sexual intimacy. The first part of the discussion will examine how sexuality

---

13. Diamond, "What We Got Wrong," 83.

14. Amnesty International, "Making Love a Crime," https://www.amnesty.org/en/documents/afr01/001/2013/en/.

is depicted in the Bible before the fall, as recorded in Genesis 1–2. The second part will explore sexuality after the fall, as recorded in the rest of the Bible.

Sexuality before the Fall

The Bible begins with the creation narrative in Genesis 1, which lays the foundation for understanding human sexuality. Genesis 1:27 states that God created humanity in his image, as male and female. While this verse does not directly refer to the innate sexual feelings inherent in males and females or the expression of sexual desires for sexual intimacy with persons of the opposite sex, it does reveal a profound truth: sexual differentiation – that is, being male or female – is a creation of God. There is no indication in the Bible that Adam and, by extension, Eve were allowed to choose their gender. According to this verse, and given the context of the creation narrative, their maleness and femaleness were not determined by personal autonomy or the roles assigned to them by society. Instead, God, without any external influence or pressure, created them as male and female.

As the narrative continues in Genesis 2, offering a more detailed account that focuses on the creation of the woman, the Bible gives us its first depiction of sexuality. After declaring that it was not good for man to be alone, God caused Adam to fall into a deep sleep and created Eve from his rib. When Adam awoke and saw Eve, he declared, "This at last is bone of my bones and flesh of my flesh; she shall be called Woman, because she was taken out of Man" (Gen 2:23 ESV). This statement indicates, to some degree, Adam's expression of desire for sexual intimacy. As mentioned earlier, the expression of sexual desires is not limited to physical actions but also involves emotional intimacy, connection, and affection between a man and a woman. This verse describes Adam building an emotional connection with Eve by referring to her as a part of himself: "bone of my bones and flesh of my flesh."

Three observations can be made about sexuality from the narrative of Genesis 1–2. First, Adam's desire to build an emotional connection with Eve was innate. When God brought Eve to Adam, there was no mention of any "creation update" that took place to enable Adam to recognize Eve as attractive. Instead, he had an innate desire to build an emotional connection with her. From the moment of Adam's creation, God had set in motion the biological processes – including genetics, hormones, and neurological factors – that worked to shape Adam's sexual attraction and drive towards Eve. Therefore, Adam required no external influence or a creation update to find Eve attractive.

The second observation is that Adam's innate sexual feelings and desires for sexual intimacy were directed towards Eve, a person of the opposite sex. This suggests that heterosexual attraction is part of God's inherent design for human sexuality. As noted earlier, the binary distinction between male and female was God's intention in creation. God not only created Adam and Eve as male and female but also hardwired them with innate sexual feelings and attraction to each other so that when Eve was brought to Adam, he naturally found her attractive and expressed his desire for intimacy with her. If God's design for human sexuality had not been intended for the opposite sex, he could have made another creature or another gender for Adam and hardwired Adam's sexual feelings and attractions so that Adam would be aroused by that creature. Instead, God created Eve for Adam – a woman for the man – signifying that the intrinsic desire for sexual intimacy is intended to be between the opposite sexes: man to woman and woman to man.

The third observation about sexuality from the Genesis 1–2 narrative is that innate sexual feelings and the desires for sexual intimacy with persons of the opposite sex are meant to be within the context of a relationship. Adam did not express his desire for sexual intimacy to a random stranger in Eden but, rather, to the woman created and brought to him by a God with whom he already had a relationship. In addition, after Adam outwardly expressed and acted upon his innate sexual feelings and desire for intimacy with Eve, the subsequent verse describes the framework for living and expressing sexuality (Gen 2:24). Using Adam and Eve as an example, the Bible declares that a man shall leave his father and mother and be united to his wife so that they can become one flesh (Gen 2:24). This signifies that when a man's sexuality is awakened by a woman, as in the case of Adam with Eve, he must leave his father and mother and be united with her in a lifelong committed relationship that we call marriage, and likewise the woman must leave her father and mother to be united with her husband in the lifelong committed relationship of marriage.

Sexuality after the Fall

With the entrance of sin due to the disobedience of Adam and Eve, human nature – including the sphere of sexuality – was adversely affected, leading to various forms of brokenness. One of the clearest and most explicit examples of the deviation from God's original plan for human sexuality is the account of Sodom and Gomorrah. In stark contrast to the heterosexual relationships established and intended by God in creation, Genesis 19 records that the inhabitants of Sodom and Gomorrah were engaging in same-sex relations.

Unfortunately, even after God destroyed Sodom and Gomorrah, sin continued to affect human sexuality. Reflecting on the pervasive impact of sin on
human sexuality, the apostle Paul, in his letter to the Romans, notes that women
exchanged natural sexual relations for unnatural ones, and men abandoned
natural relations with women, becoming inflamed with lust for one another
(Rom 1:26–27).

Another significant consequence of the fall in the area of sexuality was
the breakdown of the sanctity of marriage. As noted earlier, sexuality was
intended to be enjoyed within the context of marriage. However, after the fall,
sexuality was no longer confined to this context. Fornication and adultery were
widespread, as evidenced by numerous biblical accounts. For instance, the
story of David and Bathsheba (2 Samuel 11) illustrates how even "a man after
God's own heart" was not immune to the pervasive effects of sin on sexuality.

A Theology of Youth and Sexuality

Using insights gleaned from the biblical depiction of sexuality discussed above,
this section develops a theology of youth and sexuality. This theology posits
that sexuality, as an innate part of humanity, is assigned by God and does not
define a person's identity. Although, after the fall, sexuality has been distorted
by sin, leading to various kinds of perversions, there is hope of restoration
through Christ, who offers a path to reclaim God's original design. Therefore,
the church – and youth ministry in particular – must engage with youth compassionately, providing guidance and support as they navigate the pervasive
effects of sin on sexuality. To better understand this theology of youth and sexuality, I will break it down and explain the meaning of each phrase or sentence.

Sexuality Is Assigned to Youth by God

The biblical narrative, before the fall, asserts that sexuality, as an innate part
of human beings, is assigned to people by God. The creation of Adam, and
subsequently Eve, with their innate desire for sexual intimacy indicates that
sexuality is not a human construct but a divine endowment. In contrast to
contemporary discourse that often depicts sexuality as a social construct, the
account of Adam and Eve underscores its inherent nature. Adam's immediate
recognition of and attraction to Eve demonstrate that from the moment of his
creation, God had already established the biological processes that shaped his
sexual attraction and drive towards Eve. Therefore, Adam required no creation update from God or any external influence to find Eve sexually attractive

because God had already assigned his sexuality. This implies that for youth – just as for Adam and all humans – sexuality is not a social construct or a personal choice but something that is assigned by God.

Sexuality Does Not Define Youth's Identity

While sexuality is an integral part of human existence, it does not define a person's worth or identity. Genesis 2:18–20 suggests that Adam was a complete being before Eve's creation. In other words, his identity and relationship with God were established independently of his sexuality. This implies that human worth and identity are rooted in the *imago Dei* (the image of God) rather than in sexuality. Another biblical example that illustrates this point is found with reference to eunuchs. In Matthew 19:12, Jesus spoke of eunuchs who have been made so for the sake of the kingdom of heaven. By affirming that eunuchs are valued and significant in God's plan and kingdom, Jesus implied that sexuality is not the ultimate measure of a person's worth or identity. In other words, while sexuality is significant, it does not define human identity.

Therefore, the phrase "sexuality does not define a youth's identity" is crucial to the theology of youth and sexuality because it underscores that while sexuality is an integral part of human existence, it does not determine the entirety of a young person's worth and identity.

Sexuality Remains Distorted until Sin Is Dealt With

The biblical narrative acknowledges that sin has profoundly distorted human sexuality, leading to various forms of perversion and brokenness. Despite this pervasive distortion of sexuality – as recorded in the Bible and discussed in the previous section of this chapter – there is hope for restoration through Jesus Christ. For instance, 1 Corinthians 6:9–11 affirms that those who have succumbed to the pervasive impact of sin on sexuality by being sexually immoral can be washed, sanctified, and justified in Jesus Christ. While the transformative power of the gospel provides a path for individuals to reclaim their God-given sexuality, it is crucial that a theology of youth and sexuality includes the understanding that until sin is fully dealt with, human sexuality will remain marred.

Therefore, this theology of youth and sexuality calls the church – and youth ministry by extension – to engage compassionately with young people and their struggles with sexuality. By recognizing the pervasive impact of sin on sexuality, the church and youth ministry in Africa can provide guidance and support for youth as they navigate their sexuality in a fallen world.

The Way Forward: A Model for Engaging Youth and Sexuality in Africa

Paul's approach in 1 Corinthians 6:12–20 provides a valuable model for the African church and youth ministry in engaging with youth and sexuality. When addressing the Corinthian church about the impact of sin on their sexuality – which was evident through the prevalence of sexual immorality in Corinth – Paul begins by countering the common sayings used to justify their distorted views of sexuality. Similarly, the church and youth ministry in Africa should actively engage with and counter contemporary messages that shape young people's understanding and perception of sexuality. For example, using the biblical depiction of sexuality and the theology of youth and sexuality discussed in this chapter, they can counter the prevailing contemporary idea that sexuality is a social construct with the biblical truth that God assigns sexuality.

After countering the prevailing messages that shaped and informed the Corinthians' views of sexuality, Paul does not merely offer a counternarrative or slogan. Instead, he teaches the comprehensive truth of God's word. The African church and youth ministry can emulate this approach by resisting the temptation to respond to contemporary messages and slogans that shape and inform young people's understanding and perception of sexuality with equally simplistic phrases. Instead, like the apostle Paul, they should focus on offering biblical teaching that helps young people understand that sexuality, as an integral part of their existence, is assigned to them by God and does not define their identity.

Conclusion

The aim of this chapter is to assist the church and youth ministry in Africa to broaden their understanding on youth and sexuality and approach this topic in a more nuanced and informed way. The chapter began by defining sexuality from a biblically informed perspective as the innate sexual feelings inherent in males and females and the expression of desire for sexual intimacy with persons of the opposite sex – that is, male (man) to female (woman), and vice versa.

After outlining this biblically informed definition of sexuality, the chapter evaluated the contemporary messages that inform and shape young people's perception and understanding of sexuality in Africa. These messages include the ideas of sexuality as a social construct, sexuality as a choice, and sexuality as an identity. To equip churches and youth ministries in Africa to engage with these messages, the chapter examined how people in the Bible expressed their sexuality. In light of that, the chapter developed a theology of youth and sexuality that asserts that sexuality is assigned to youth by God and does not define their identity. However, the church and youth ministry are called to compassionately provide guidance and support for youth as they navigate their sexuality in a fallen world.

Discussion Questions

1.   Why is it essential to view sexuality as assigned by God rather than as a personal choice?

2.   How can understanding that sexuality does not define a person help in ministering to young people who are struggling with their sexuality?

3.   How should the church address the ongoing distortions of human sexuality due to sin?

4.   How can youth ministries effectively counter contemporary messages about sexuality with biblical truth?

5.   How can the theology of youth and sexuality outlined in this chapter help churches and youth ministries to engage more effectively with youth on the topic of sexuality?

6.   How can the church and youth ministries implement the model outlined in this chapter for engaging youth on the topic of sexuality?

Bibliography

Amnesty International. "Making Love a Crime: Criminalization of Same-Sex Conduct in Sub-Saharan Africa." 2013. https://www.amnesty.org/en/documents/afr01/001/2013/en/.

Berger, Peter, and Thomas Luckmann. "The Social Construction of Reality." In *Social Theory Re-Wired*, edited by Wesley Longhofer and Daniel Winchester, 110–22. New York: Routledge, 2016.

Butler, Judith. *Gender Trouble: Feminism and the Subversion of Identity*. New York: Routledge, 2006.

Closson, David. *Biblical Principles for Human Sexuality: Survey of Culture, Scripture, and Church History*. USA: Family Research Council, 2022.

DeLamater, John, and William N. Friedrich. "Human Sexual Development." *Journal of Sex Research* 39, no. 1 (2002): 10–14.

Diamond, Lisa M. "What We Got Wrong about Sexual Identity Development: Unexpected Findings from a Longitudinal Study of Young Women." In *Sexual Orientation and Mental Health: Examining Identity and Development in Lesbian, Gay, and Bisexual People*, edited by Allen M. Omoto and Howard S. Kurtzman, 73–94. Washington, DC: American Psychological Association, 2006. https://doi.org/10.1037/11261-004.

Durkheim, Emile. "The Elementary Forms of Religious Life." In *Social Theory Re-Wired*, edited by Wesley Longhofer and Daniel Winchester, 52–67. New York: Routledge, 2016.

Foucault, Michel. *The History of Sexuality: An Introduction*. Vol. 1 of *The History of Sexuality*. Translated by Robert Hurley. New York: Vintage Books, 1990.

Kok, E. L. "Sexuality: How It Is Defined and Determined?" *South African Family Practice* 46, no. 3 (2004): 39–42.

Magnuson, Ken. *Invitation to Christian Ethics*. Grand Rapids: Kregel Academic, 2020.

Mogoatlhe, Lerato. "Why Women in Zambia's Capital Joined the Women's March." *Global Citizen*, 24 January 2020. https://www.globalcitizen.org/en/content/womens-march-movement-lusaka-2020/.

Muehlenhard, Charlene L., and Zoe D. Peterson. "Distinguishing between Sex and Gender: History, Current Conceptualizations, and Implications." *Sex Roles* 64 (2011): 791–803.

Petrey, Taylor G. "Theology of Sexuality." In *The Routledge Handbook of Mormonism and Gender*, edited by Amy Hoyt and Taylor G. Petrey, 509–24. New York: Routledge, 2020.

Pryzgoda, Jayde, and Joan C. Chrisler. "Definitions of Gender and Sex: The Subtleties of Meaning." *Sex Roles* 43 (2000): 553–69.

Siann, Gerda. *Gender, Sex and Sexuality: Contemporary Psychological Perspectives*. London: Taylor & Francis, 2013. https://doi.org/10.4324/9780203992562.

Unger, Rhoda K., and Mary Crawford. "Sex and Gender: The Troubled Relationship between Terms and Concepts." *Psychological Science* 4, no. 2 (1993): 122–24.

2

Youth and Culture

Kevin Muriithi Ndereba

The World of Youth: A Changing Landscape

One of the most widely read blog pages in an East African country captures the twenty-first-century world with these words:

> You will never find me standing in the middle of the room. I'm that guy who stalks the borders of a room. I belong in the darkened embrace of the shadows. The problem with standing in the middle of the room is that you become part of the narrative and there the power to tell the story of that room is perpetually stripped off you. And so I'm the guy who relishes watching that narrative unspool from those borders of the room. Then capture it in words; the best seat in the room is where there are no seats. I love music, food, travel, children (even those that don't belong to me), clothes, cars, gadgets, whiskey and watching someone hula-hoop. There is something defeatist about that thing, like a dog trying to bite its own tail. But more than loving all the aforementioned, I love to write about these things.[1]

Jackson Biko is a Kenyan writer whose Facebook page attracts more than 90,000 followers, primarily young people. Biko rose to fame through his narrative writing style that captured the untold, yet relatable stories of Kenyan people. From stories of young people being made tribal chiefs, to how people got involved with drug addiction and came out of it, to stories of untold genocide and rape, Biko evokes the capacity of using the new technologies

---

1. Bikozulu, http://www.bikozulu.co.ke/.

to connect human narratives. Yet, while many of these stories capture the human aspects of everyday life, they remain encapsulated in worldviews such as hedonism, relativism and existentialism. Ministry leaders are invited to reflect on how the story of redemption can speak to these everyday examples of young people immersed in popular culture of social media.

Technology and New Media

Whereas most African baby boomers (those born in the 1960s) spent their youth in villages and plantation fields, millennial youth (those born in the 1990s) spend most of their time in the virtual world. While the baby boomers inherited their values through the oral tradition in their communities, millennials are drowning in a sea of disparate views in the online world. In other words, their definition of who they are is a blend of alternatives that decries any objective definition. They are attracted to a virtual world of fantasy – a world that offers the joys of relational intimacy without the heart values that provide a solid foundation. In this world, many young people feel a sense of community, a liturgical space where they can worship – worship the created but not the Creator. However, all is not gloomy.

Safaricom is one of the most formidable telecommunications companies in the African market. Its software application MPESA has broken the glass ceiling of the African economy by penetrating global markets, catapulting this local brand to become a global and respected name. MPESA has helped many people to transact money for the acquisition of essential goods and services. YouTube has created an "information village" with easy access to and creation of content that is beneficial to learners. It is through this online market that educational institutions are offering Open Distance Learning (ODeL) to tap into this new world of the millennials – education that is affordable and flexible, meeting the dynamic needs of a mobile generation. Despite its perils, social media still remains a remarkable tool for learning, teaching, creating, collaborating, and exchanging ideas. Technology and new media are breaking down geographical boundaries, increasing the interaction of cultures and worldviews, and influencing a variety of fields such as sociology, religion, and economics. As a result of this transition, traditional boundaries have become blurred or almost non-existent, leading to the phenomenon of globalization and its attendant cultural context of postmodernism.[2]

Globalization and Postmodernity

The reality of globalization can be examined from various perspectives. In short, globalization refers to "the intensification of worldwide interconnectivity, mobility, and imagination."[3] The scholar Manfred Steger proposes that globalization is multifaceted and encompasses economic, political, cultural, ecological, and religious dimensions.[4] He notes that although globalization can be traced back to the 1930s, it became a buzzword in the 1990s due to the penetration of Information and Communications Technology (ICT) and integration of markets. With the genesis of these multifaceted factors, such an integration would lead to a connected world, with multiple perspectives and the obscuring of objective values. One can see how this increased integration can easily result in the blurring of definitions, which some scholars refer to as postmodernism.

It is a common experience for youth workers to encounter conversations like this:

"What do you think about dating a girl who is not of the same faith as you are?" asks a concerned youth worker.

"I can't really explain clearly. I think it depends . . . ," replies the sincere youth leader, who has been attending the youth ministry for a year now.

Concerned about the lack of a clear definition, the youth worker presses on: "It depends on . . .?"

"Well," begins the puzzled youth leader, "it depends. It depends on whether she has good values. It may also depend on whether she

---

2. During my paper presentation on "Relational Apologetics for African Youth Ministry" during the International Association for the Study of Youth Ministry (IASYM) held on Sep 6–8, 2018 which was finally published as Ndereba, Kevin Muriithi, "Ubuntu apologetics in faith formation: An ethnography of youth ministry in Nairobi," *Journal of Youth and Theology* 21, no. 2 (2021): 107–22, Prof. Reginald Nel, Dean and Missiology Professor, Stellenbosch University raised a critical observation on postmodernity. He proposed that postmodernity in the African context needs to be critiqued and nuanced. The reason is that it is developed in the European historical context of modernity and needs to be rethought especially for Africa's historical and contemporary context.

3. Steger, *Globalization*, Introduction.

4. Steger, *Globalization*, 1.

is willing to consider changing faiths. It depends on whether she makes me happy. It depends on many things," he finally answers.

Although the youth worker presses for an objective, clear-cut definition, the youth leader remains subjective. One sees here the confluence of the various issues mentioned earlier. The integration of religious traditions in a cosmopolitan and pluralistic environment presents unique challenges in practical areas of life. In the current postmodern climate, many young people find it difficult to define their values, assess truth claims, and depend on the sufficiency of Scripture. Citing late-twentieth-century scholars of culture such as David Harvey, Zygmunt Bauman, and Ulrich Beck, Paul Hodkinson and Wolfgang Deicke note that postmodern theory is concerned with fragmentation and fluidity, which contrasts with modernity's stability, certainty, and sense of community.[5] However, this "cultural exile" presents an opportunity for Christianity. James K. Smith, a Christian philosopher and minister, argues that it is only a "robust, vibrant and liturgical church" that can offer true meaning in the anti-institutional spirituality of postmodern culture.[6] However, in this blurry cultural climate, youth workers frequently encounter the same subjective blurriness among the young people they work with. How does this affect how young people view their world – that is, their *worldview*?

In his helpful handbook on worldviews, James Sire notes that worldviews are assumptions or presuppositions that people hold, consciously or subconsciously, and that these presuppositions, which may be tested or untested, concern the make-up of reality.[7] The main elements of a worldview include epistemology (questions about knowledge), ethics (right and wrong), metaphysics (reality), aesthetics (beauty, arts and music), and sociology (identity formation). If Western modernity could be described as a period of stability, then postmodernity can be seen as a harbinger of instability, bringing up questions of knowledge such as "What is the basis of knowledge?" In addition, ideas like "my truth is not your truth" mean that truth cannot be verified, which challenges the concept of objective truth. Second, the underlying assumption that "what is right for me may be wrong for you" makes it problematic

---

5. Hodkinson and Deicke, *Youth Cultures*, 8.

6. Smith, *Who's Afraid of Postmodernism?*, 11. The subtitle, *Taking Derrida, Lyotard and Foucault to Church*, captures the history of postmodernity, originating from French philosophical currents in existentialism and influencing fields as diverse as art, architecture, and film. Stanley Grenz, a theologian and ethicist, observes that postmodernity tries to counter the intellectual foundations of modernity – that is, objectivity, certainty, and goodness of knowledge. Grenz, *Primer on Postmodernism*, 2.

7. Sire, *Universe Next Door*, 20.

to respond to moral issues, especially in areas such as sexuality (for example, sexual identity and practice) and ethical life issues (for example, abortion and euthanasia). Third, the line between fantasy and reality is obscured when young people's actions are influenced by the video games they play and the sexual content they consume on social media. Issues such as gambling, violence, and pornography are symptomatic of this postmodern deluge influencing youth culture. Finally, aesthetics and sociology may impact self-esteem, leading to identity crises and social repression. In essence, globalization, which may be viewed as the melting pot of postmodernity, contributes to the recession of Christian values from the public sphere.

Secularization in Popular Culture

One of the most influential books concerning the topic of secularism in an African context was written by Aylward Shorter,[8] a Catholic missiologist who studied how Christian theology was inculturated or appropriated in Africa. Shorter challenges John Mbiti's claim that "Africans are religious" by arguing that the overemphasis on economic consumerism and its propagation through media is rooted in a "western culture that is intrinsically divisive and imperialist."[9] In Shorter's view, such a culture promotes a privatized form of religion that cannot effectively address the separation of the secular and the sacred, thereby pushing religious values – particularly Christian values – to the periphery of the public sphere.

In contemporary Kenya's public sphere, several organizations are at the forefront of such a secularizing agenda. For instance, Atheists in Kenya Society seeks to challenge religious fundamentalism and has, on several occasions in the past (in 2018), advocated for legislation to remove religious education from primary schools. The Gay and Lesbian Coalition of Kenya are seeking human rights in the area of gender and sexual orientation by partnering with governmental, non-governmental, and civic organizations and institutions such as the Kenya National Commission on Human Rights (KNCHR), which recently issued a statement arguing that discrimination against sexual orientation – which has often been a consequence of religious and cultural opinions – is not supported by Article 27(4) of Kenya's constitution.[10] While human rights are

---

8. Shorter, *Secularism in Africa*.

9. Shorter, *Secularism in Africa*.

10. KNCHR, https://www.knchr.org/Articles/ArtMID/2432/ArticleID/1068/Press-Relea-seInternational-Day-Against-HomophobiaBiphobiaInterphobia-and-TransphobiaIDAHOBIT.

theologically embedded in the *imago Dei*, what might these legislative pressures mean for youth and sexuality? In what ways might Christian institutions and churches offer a loving response that honours God's holy character and, going forward, facilitates transformation? When engaging with such cultural issues, there are three possible views that Christians may adopt: accommodation, isolation, or transformation.[11] Accommodation allows a secular agenda to be pursued by those who may be seeking to "dethrone" God in the public sphere. This approach concedes that we can pursue human rights without reference to God or a biblical worldview. At the other extreme is isolation, which resembles the approach of the earliest Christian communities such as the Essenes or other fundamentalists groups in Christian history who, in their pursuit of purity, simplistically withdrew entirely from the public sphere. The third option is wise transformation through public engagement by means of dialogue, policy-making, and rebuttals that are informed by a comprehensive biblical worldview. The next section will explore how this can be done.

The case made so far is that secularization theory significantly shapes popular culture, which presents unique challenges for the Christian mission. However, all is not lost. While secularization theories in the Western world were often aimed at "dethroning God" by emphasizing the influence of modernity on faith or religious identity, the present resurgence of religious movements, including Christianity, offers a different view. One sociologist moves beyond the simplistic secularization theory that modernity leads to religious disaffiliation by observing that secularization and resurgence of faith can occur concurrently.[12] In fact, Christianity is steadily growing; and many observers note that within the developing world, the centre of faith is shifting towards the Global South. Between 1910 and 2010, a period of a century, the number of Christians increased from six hundred million to about two billion. According to projections from the Pew Forum, the number of Christians is expected to reach 3.1 billion by 2060 (with the number of Muslims also growing to about the same figure, just 1 percent less than the total Christian population).[13] Similarly, scholars from the Gordon-Conwell Center for Global Christianity note that while Christianity is declining in Europe, Latin America, and Northern America due to slow population growth, it is growing significantly in the Asian

---

11. Mburu, "Leadership," 3–19.

12. Riesebrodt, "Religion in the Modern World," 1–15.

13. Pew Research Center, "Changing Global Religious Landscape," *Religion and Public Life*, 5 April 2017.

and African continents due to higher population growth rates.[14] These statistics present an opportunity for youth workers to rethink the global influence of their Christian work. In the next section, we will examine biblical-theological reflections on some of these issues and consider their practical implications for youth ministry.

The Word: Biblical-Theological Reflections on *Missio Dei* and Youth

The previous section provided a broad overview of youth and culture. Despite the "global youth culture" brought about by the "shrinking" of the technological world, there still remain some unique local youth cultures.[15] Scholars of adolescent development note that contrary to some of the previously mentioned generalizations about youth, some young people are outliers in relation to some of the issues of Westernization, fashion, sexual identity, and media. Some examples include arranged marriages that are agreeable to many Asian youth, street youth in some East African countries who develop a niche in urban environments, the physical separation of school-going boys and girls in the Middle East, Russian youth who are marrying earlier in order to legitimize sexual unions, and Mexican women who face societal pressures to marry and have children in their early twenties. In summary, though the twenty-first century presents unique sociocultural forces, each young person is affected in unique ways. This aligns with the understanding that each person is created in the image of God (Gen 1:26; Ps 139:13–16). This section argues that a biblical theology of *missio Dei* (God's mission) presents a robust framework for youth work.

The biblical-theological approach takes into serious consideration the sweep of any particular theme throughout Scripture. It seeks to be faithful to God's word by taking a panoramic view of the Scriptures, from which individual principles and applications can be derived. A biblical theology of *missio Dei* traces God's mission activity from Genesis to Revelation. Tracing this theme through the biblical canon reveals the following key issues:

1. God's mission begins with his creative acts in the Genesis account (Genesis 1).

---

14. Johnson et al., "Christianity in Its Global Context."
15. Brown, Larson, and Saraswathi, *World's Youth*, 2.

2. In response to the fall, God's mission is to reconcile humanity through the Christological "seed" who will crush the serpent's "head" (Gen 3:15).

3. In Old Testament Jewish history, God's mission includes calling an individual (Abraham) and a nation (Israel) to display his glory.

4. In exilic history, God's mission involves judgement, justice, preservation, and the promise of redemption for his people.

5. In the New Testament, God's mission finds fulfilment in the person of Jesus Christ, who is "Abraham's seed."

6. Those who belong to God's family by faith are gathered – both locally and globally – into the church, whose mission is to participate in God's "Great Commission" through evangelism, discipleship, and mission.

7. The final climactic act of God's mission is the restoration and renewal of his creation in the final victory over sin, Satan, and evil.

Such a biblical theology views young people as created in the image of God. This gives youth workers a foundation upon which to affirm young people and call them back to this God-given value and identity. In the fall, this goodness is marred and affects the very nature of young people. Their participation in risky or hedonistic behaviour, cultural relativism, and confusion as they develop is merely an outworking of the reality of sin. In the post-2008 reality of an economic crisis, youth have been viewed with suspicion and treated as suspects in their resistance to socio-economic and political status quos. Henry Giroux eloquently observes that "young people have become a generation of suspects in a society destroyed by the merging of market fundamentalism, consumerism, and militarism" and that their guardians continue to respond with indifference, disrespect, and abandon.[16] This "marginality and disposability" of youth echoes Israel's exilic experiences. How might youth workers today exercise a prophetic role, calling people to reformation and revival like Nehemiah, Ezra, and their Old Testament contemporaries? In this "dry and thirsty land," is there no "balm in Gilead"? Youth workers have an opportunity to participate in the *missio Dei* among those they serve by speaking equally about justice and restoration, as well as about peril and promise that is centred on the "suffering servant" in the writings of Isaiah (Isaiah 52 and 53). The New Testament presents transformative images of young people and youth work

---

16. Giroux, *Youth in a Suspect Society*, 31.

that are grounded in the *missio Dei*. Jesus welcomed children and youth, and these young people are identified as Christians in the family baptisms described in Acts, while young leaders such as Titus and Timothy are commended and commissioned in the Epistles. From this broad exploration of the biblical theology of *missio Dei*, the following conclusions can be drawn for youth work:

1. God calls youth workers to engage in his multifaceted mission, which includes affirming the image of God in young people, prophetically lamenting the distortions in youth culture and systemic structures that marginalize them, and graciously proclaiming the gospel to them. This may involve vision casting, administration, discipleship, preaching, proclamation, evangelism, and apologetics, all of which are central to the task of practical theology.

2. Since young people are created in the image of God, youth workers can connect with them by using elements of popular culture – such as music, movies, and media – that celebrate the good in the lives of these youth.[17]

3. The reality of the fall invites us to seriously consider not only outward behaviours but also the sin nature. Youth workers must remember that the battle is bigger than their own methods or strength (Eph 6:10–20).

4. Young people can be truly transformed only through a saving, personal relationship with Jesus Christ and the ministry of the Holy Spirit in their lives.

5. Youth work should focus on redemption rather than perfection. This takes into serious consideration what Christ has already done and what he will bring to completion when he returns or calls us home. This is the "already but not yet" model that biblical theologians refer to when they remind us that God's mission has a climactic end (1 John 3:2).

---

17. Compare with Paul's engagement with the Athenians in Acts 17:16–34. His model of "bridge building" from the unknown to the known, shows the need of being aware of some of the cultural influencers such as musicians, poets and social media influencers. Paul uses this awareness of Athenian cultural influencers and ideas, to then engage them with the Judeo-Christian worldview.

The Way Forward: Engaging African Youth Culture

Paul's engagement with the Athenians in Acts 17 provides a biblical model for engaging with culture. As noted earlier, the three options for cultural engagement can be described, very simply, as accommodation, isolation, and transformation. Accommodation involved "conforming" to the ideologies and ways of the world (Rom 12:2). At the other extreme, isolation is complete detachment from the world – this is contrary to Scripture, which teaches us to be in the world but not of it, to be salt and light, and to live in the world but have our citizenship in heaven (Matt 5:13–16; Col 3:15–17; Phil 3:17–21). In Acts 17, Paul's approach to cultural engagement is transformation. To achieve holistic transformation of youth culture for Christ, we can break down Paul's approach into two key steps, which are described in the section below.

Cultural Immersion and Engagement

How can youth practitioners immerse themselves in culture while maintaining a robust Christian witness? Stephen Bevans, Charles Kraft, and Richard Niebuhr offer several frameworks for cultural immersion. Bevans, a Roman Catholic missiologist, presents his models of contextualization on a spectrum, with the two extremes of *translation* and *anthropological* models and a *synthetic* model in the middle. All theology is contextual in nature as it engages Scripture, ecclesiological tradition, and culture. The *translation* model is heavily influenced by Scripture, the *anthropological* model by culture, and the *synthetic* model seeks to balance the three models.[18] In Bevans' model of cultural engagement, youth practitioners must consider biblical theology, youth culture, and Christian tradition. Overemphasizing any one of these aspects destabilizes this "three-legged stool" that is vital for effective ministry to young people. Depending on any single model is short-sighted and may fail to bring about any meaningful gospel-cultural change, as articulated by one theologian who engages with Bevans' model:

> The strength of translation approaches again is their insistence on the content of the gospel message. Maintaining this emphasis should keep us from minimizing the centrality of Scripture, or of placing culture on a par with the Bible as a source of revelation, as anthropological models do.[19]

---

18. See Bevans, *Models of Contextual Theology*.
19. Stabell, "Rethinking Contextualization," 165–78.

We may say that, on the surface, the interplay of media, peers, and guardians impacts two levels in the cultural microcosm of young people, in line with Kraft's thinking: *Surface-Level Culture* (outward patterns of behaviour) and *Deep-Level Culture* (worldview assumptions).[20] Factors such as dress, hairstyles, and behavioural patterns may serve as outward indicators of deeper assumptions about God, identity, and sexuality. The main challenge in engaging with youth culture is in finding ways to communicate the gospel to young people without imposing our own cultural assumptions on them.[21] In his book *Christianity in Culture: A Study in Biblical-Theologizing in Cross-Cultural Perspective*, Kraft seems to borrow from the work of the theologian Richard Niebuhr.[22] Niebuhr proposes five models of the interrelationship between Christ and culture, but I mention here the three that stand out: *Christ against Culture* lies at one extreme, seeing all cultural expressions outside Christianity as opposed to the gospel; *Christ of Culture* sees no tension between Christ and culture; and *Christ Transforming Culture* recognizes both positive and negative elements and rightly acknowledges the tensions between the gospel message and culture. Paul's approach in Acts 17, as well as in his interactions with Jews and Gentiles, reflects elements of each of these approaches. For instance, his insistence that he knows nothing but Christ crucified (1 Cor 2:2) demonstrates his heavy leaning on the "Christ against Culture" and "translation" models described above. On the other hand, his becoming "all things to all people" (1 Cor 9:19–23) illustrates the "anthropological" and "Christ for Culture" models. Therefore, we may conclude that spiritual discernment is essential for navigating different situations in the practice of youth ministry. The *telos* or end goal of ministry is conformity to Christlikeness, which is transformation that leads to the right worship of God.

Spiritual Deconstruction and Reconstruction

The purpose of being immersed in youth culture is to understand the signs and symbols at play since these surface-level issues often give us insight into deeper-level issues. After cultural immersion, the second phase is spiritual deconstruction and reconstruction, which may be defined as the process of spiritual assessment of the practical issue and applying the mind of Christ with the aim of wholeness. The deeper-level issues result in a tension stemming

---

20. Kraft, "Culture, Worldview and Contextualization," 384–91.

21. Kraft.

22. Kraft, *Christianity in Culture*, and Niebuhr, *Christ and Culture*.

from both agreement and disagreement with the Judeo-Christian worldview. In Paul's encounter at Athens (Acts 17:16–34), several Athenian beliefs aligned with his own Christian convictions: (1) they were religious (17:22), as per the Augustinian view of the sense of the divine; (2) they had a sense of worship (17:23); (3) they recognized God's immanence (17:27–28); and (4) they had some idea about spiritual regeneration (17:27). On the other hand, the following were in conflict with Paul's Christian convictions: (1) they worshipped idols; (2) they had a false understanding of knowledge, as demonstrated by the response of the Stoic and Epicurean philosophers; (3) they mistakenly viewed Jesus as one among many gods (17:18; compare 17:29, 31); and (4) they did not fully grasp the reality of righteousness, spiritual regeneration, and judgement (17:30–31). Paul's central message, which should also be our message, is the resurrection of Jesus Christ (17:32; 1 Cor 15:3–4), which lies at the heart of Christianity and underscores its distinctiveness in a multi-faith world. Youth practitioners must be aware that their message, like Paul's message to the Athenians and other audiences, will frequently give rise to two contrasting responses (17:32–34).

Gospel Transformation and the Church

D. A. Carson critiques Niebuhr, arguing that we have taken his liberal approach to Scripture and canonized his models as the only method for Christian engagement with culture. While acknowledging that these models can be beneficial, Carson contends that a return to biblical theology – which has been the emphasis of this chapter – is vital for critically engaging with the complexities of youth culture.[23] In Carson's own words,

> These turning points in the history of redemption must shape Christian thinking about the relationships between Christ and culture. The structures generated by such biblical theology are robust enough to allow the many differing emphases within Scripture to find their voices, so that to speak of different "models" of the Christ-and-culture relationship begins to look misleading.[24]

As Christians living in the post-Pentecost era, biblical theology must be central to our understanding of and response to the topic of youth and culture. The church that began in Jerusalem carries the gospel entrusted to it to the

23. Carson, *Christ and Culture Revisited*.
24. Carson, preface.

ends of the earth. The message of the gospel is contextualized for increasingly divergent audiences (Acts 13:16–41; 14:15–17; 17:22–31) to facilitate the spiritual unity and ethnical diversity of the church of Christ (15:1–35) for the ultimate worship of the Father, Son, and Holy Spirit.[25] In summary, the book of Acts offers us a template for cultural inclusion that is centered on the ministry and complete work of the Triune God. For contemporary Christians, the following paragraph reflected the necessity of ethnic unity as part of our expression of being united in Christ:

> Today church life tends to be fragmented or distorted by the constraints of modern culture. Acts gives us a welcome pattern of balance and wholeness, showing how spiritual characteristics such as love, joy and unity were lived out in mutual ministry to the whole person. That wholeness extended to racial and ethnic relations, with the challenge to visibly express oneness in Christ.[26]

Only the church of Jesus Christ can provide the necessary context for young people to grow in community, embracing their uniqueness while also standing on the timeless truths of past generations of faithful believers. Youth practitioners have the opportunity to engage with cultural influencers such as Sauti Sol and Bikozulu while remaining rooted in a robust biblical theology that takes into consideration the eschatological end in light of specific cultural experiences. This undertaking by youth workers is an important way of bearing witness to the transforming power of God the Father, realized by God the Son, and applied by God the Spirit. It is vital that youth ministry is founded on the bedrock of sound theology:

> We all need reminders that practical ministry and practical theology flow from God and are intricately connected to each other. This is an awesome truth beyond proof to the skeptical or distracted mind. The Creator's love and grace initiate the relationship and partnership God desires with humans. Our inclination to love a neighbor and to serve a younger generation is of God; effective ministry is letting God love and bless through us. It is God who has put the compassion and desire to care in our hearts.[27]

---

25. Carson, 189.
26. Carson, 14
27. Borgman, *Foundations for Youth Ministry.*

Beginning with God's self-revelation, there is hope "for understanding the origin and nature of culture and obvious dilemmas in culture, and to comprehend the hope of human redemption."[28] This is the basis of Kenda Dean's provocative question to any committed youth minister: "Have we built ministry on theological bedrock, or on the shifting sand of cultural relevance?"[29] In youth ministry today, a strong focus on biblical theology is crucial for deep-level cultural engagement with young people.[30]

Discussion Questions

1. In what ways have technology and new media shaped youth culture today?

2. How has globalization, postmodernity, and secularization influenced youth and culture?

3. Why is it important to view youth ministry through the biblical-theological lens of *missio Dei*?

4. What is the role of cultural immersion in effectively engaging youth and culture?

5. Why is a sound biblical theology essential for youth ministry as the basis for any deep-level cultural engagement?

Bibliography

Bevans, Stephen B. *Models of Contextual Theology.* Maryknoll: Orbis Books, 1999.

Borgman, Dean. *Foundations for Youth Ministry: Theological Engagement with Teen Life and Culture.* Grand Rapids: Baker, 2013.

Brown, B. Bradford, Reed W. Larson, and T. S. Saraswathi, eds. *The World's Youth: Adolescence in Eight Regions of the Globe.* Cambridge: Cambridge University Press, 2004.

---

28. Borgman, 8.

29. Dean, Clark, and Rahn, *Starting Right.*

30. For four approaches to youth ministry, see Senter et al., *Four Views.* The *missional approach* sees youth and youth pastors as missionaries to the culture; the *preparatory approach* sees adolescents and young adults as disciples-in-training to lead the church of the future; the *strategic approach* sees youth ministry as a potential church plant or new church, and thus the youth ministry and its leaders as built and commissioned to lead a daughter church of the mother church; and the *inclusive-congregational approach* sees youth as fully integrated in the life of the community.

Carson, D. A. *Christ and Culture Revisited*. Grand Rapids: Eerdmans, 2008.

Dean, Kenda Creasy, Chap Clark, and David Rahn, eds. *Starting Right: Thinking Theologically about Youth Ministry*. Grand Rapids: Zondervan, 2001.

Giroux, Henry A. *Youth in a Suspect Society: Democracy or Disposability?* New York: Palgrave Macmillan, 2009.

Grenz, Stanley J. *A Primer on Postmodernism*. Grand Rapids: Eerdmans, 1996.

Hodkinson, Paul, and Wolfgang Deicke, eds. *Youth Cultures: Scenes, Subcultures and Tribes*. New York; London: Routledge, 2007.

Center for the Study of Global Christianity. "Christianity in Its Global Context, 1970–2020: Society, Religion, and Mission." Gordon-Conwell Center for the Study of Global Christianity. South Hamilton: Center for the Study of Global Christianity, 2013.

Kraft, Charles. *Christianity in Culture: A Study in Biblical-Theologizing in Cross-Cultural Perspective*. Maryknoll: Orbis Books, 2005.

———. "Culture, Worldview and Contextualization." In *Perspectives on the World Christian Movement: A Reader*, edited by Ralph D. Winter and Steven C. Hawthorne, 384–91. Pasadena: William Carey Library, 1999.

Mburu, Elizabeth. "Leadership – Isolation, Absorption or Engagement: Paul, the Paradigmatic Role Model." *African Journal of Evangelical Theology* 32 (2013): 3–19.

Niebuhr, H. Richard. *Christ and Culture*. New York: Harper & Row, 1951.

Pew Research Center. "The Changing Global Religious Landscape." *Religion and Public Life*, 5 April 2017.

Riesebrodt, Martin. "Religion in the Modern World: Between Secularization and Resurgence." Max Weber Lecture delivered at the European University Institute 1. 2014.

Senter, Mark H., III, Wesley Black, Chap Clark, and Malan Nel. *Four Views of Youth Ministry and the Church: Inclusive Congregational, Preparatory, Missional, Strategic*. Grand Rapids: Zondervan, 2001.

Shorter, Aylward. *Secularism in Africa: A Case Study: Nairobi City*. Nairobi: Paulines Publications Africa, 1997.

———. "Secularism in Africa: Introducing the Problem." *African Christian Studies* 13, no. 1 (1997): 3–11.

Sire, James W. *The Universe Next Door: A Basic Worldview Catalog*. 5th ed. Downers Grove: InterVarsity Press 2009.

Smith, James K. A. *Who's Afraid of Postmodernism: Taking Derrida, Lyotard and Foucault to Church*. Grand Rapids: Baker Academic, 2006.

Stabell, Timothy D. "Rethinking Contextualization and the Gospel in Africa." *Africa Journal of Evangelical Theology* 24, no. 2 (2005): 165–78.

Steger, Manfred, Roland Benedikter, Harald Pechlaner, and Ingrid Kofler, eds. *Globalization: Past, Present, Future*. University of California Press, 2023. Accessed February 17, 2025. https://www.perlego.com/book/4266668.

Online Resources

https://www.knchr.org/Articles/ArtMID/2432/ArticleID/1068/Press-ReleaseInternational-Day-Against-HomophobiaBiphobiaInterphobia-and-TransphobiaIDAHOBIT.

Bikozulu. Accessed on 28 June, 2018. http://www.bikozulu.co.ke/.

3

Youth and Spirituality in Africa

Shantelle Weber

Introduction

The theological interpretations of denominational faith traditions have played an important role in how people understand spirituality. An understanding of the theological backgrounds of these faith traditions is important to appreciate the impact of various practices on people's perceptions of spirituality. Africa is home to a variety of theological, religious, and cultural faith traditions, each contributing to distinct practices and understandings of spirituality. Christian spirituality must be distinguished from other forms of spirituality. Spirituality is our human response to our yearning for meaning, identity, connection, and surrender. Unless this spirituality is holistic, it will be limited to a dualistic perception of self that separates our spirituality from the rest of our lives. Christian spirituality is dependent on the Holy Spirit for wholeness. This chapter is part of a broader endeavor to grapple with what a "Biblical Theology of Youth Ministry" looks like among African youth.

It is against this background that we will consider the diverse cultural and religious perceptions of spirituality that influence young people, with the aim of exploring how the Christian faith as a practice of spirituality should be taken seriously within youth ministry in Africa. A distinction will be made between traditional and modern African spirituality. Christian spirituality, like the Christian faith, involves more than just knowing about God and calls for a search for meaning. Youth in Africa are developing on varying levels, and this chapter argues that the spirituality of these youth has to be prioritized if the church in Africa is to grow beyond current generations. The chapter also elaborates on how African spirituality shapes these young people's understanding of the gospel and their ability to discern truth in postmodern Africa. The main focus will be on youth in urban contexts.

My hope is that this chapter would be relevant for youth workers, pastors, and teachers who journey alongside young people facing tensions between understanding the value of their traditional African heritage while seeking to serve Christ as they live in postmodern cities.

A Brief History of Christianity in Africa

In postmodern Africa, a key topic of discussion is the issue of decolonization. Africans are reclaiming their indigenous heritage on various levels in efforts to remain true to their identity as Africans. In my view, it is not possible to write about African spirituality without reflecting on some of the tensions surrounding the history of Christianity on this continent. Perceptions of when and how Christianity began are at the core of some of the decolonization debates, which tend to prioritize colonial (Western) voices while marginalizing indigenous African voices. Since young people are frequently unaware of this history, this chapter focuses on how this knowledge can be passed on to them through youth ministry.

Africans believe that Christianity first arrived in North Africa during the first or early second century AD, which would place North African Christians among the earliest in the world.[1] From there, it slowly spread westwards from Alexandria and eastwards to Ethiopia. Michael observes that Christianity was active in Egypt, Tunisia and Ethiopia by the third century.[2] African leaders like Tertullian, Clement of Alexandria, Origen of Alexandria, Cyprian, Athanasius, and Augustine of Hippo were influential in this early development of Christianity. Although many church history books only focus on the eighteenth and nineteenth centuries – which was when Western missionaries came to Africa – Michael and Motty argue that Christianity in Africa today is founded on what took place in North Africa a millennium and a half ago.

Taiwo encourages exposing young people to the historical contributions of Africans before colonialism. He argues that African voices were marginalized as a result of Christian mission because Africans accepted not only the faith of the missionaries but also their way of life. Taiwo says that African's contributions are often not acknowledged because racism in education has taught

---

1. Motty, *Indigenous Christian Disciple-Making*, 13–14.
2. Michael, *Christian Theology*, 3.

that all significant knowledge comes from the West.[3] Parker and Wimberly agree that this marginalization of African voices has impacted how we read the Bible, our view of Jesus, our lack of appreciation for our heritage, and our view of self. They argue that:

> Many Eurocentric church officials and scholars still ignore the contributions of black people. They have accepted an image of Jesus that was created by the dominant culture and resist other images that may be more representative of their own experiences and culture . . . The presence and contribution of black people, not only in the Bible but also throughout history, have devalued, dehumanized, and denied. This reality has perpetuated black people's self-hatred, lack of respect for one another, black-on-black violence, and a systematic denial of black personhood.[4]

This lack of understanding of who we are and where we come from is evident in the lives of many young people. The call for a recognition of a Black Jesus is also evidence of the ongoing debate about our Christian history. However, Bediako cautions that the image of Africa and Africans as inherently inferior to Europe and Europeans that was prevalent in nineteenth-century Europe did not originate with the missionary movement but with earlier conquests that enslaved Africans.[5] The African identity problem is a result of the European impact on Africa. He notes that the early spread of Christianity in the first and second centuries brought with it Christians who were proponents of slavery and racial discrimination as a means of enhancing Western economic interests. For many Africans, "denying self" meant giving up their cultural heritage in the name of Christianity. Christianity has often "been fashioned and shaped to meet the needs and aspirations of the Western church and to impose the heritage of the Enlightenment period."[6] Bediako encourages youth today to take up the challenge of accurately reshaping church history. This can only happen if young people understand who they are spiritually, and this spirituality should be rooted in a Christian theology that acknowledges the various cultural and religious traditions that impact our faith.[7] "The African context must reprocess or reconstruct Christian theology in order to address African

---

3. Táíwò, Unpublished public lecture (University of the West Indies, Mona, May 15, 2009).
4. Wimberly and Parker, *In Search of Wisdom*, 42.
5. Bediako, *Christianity in Africa*, 5–7.
6. Michael, *Christian Theology*, xvi.
7. Bediako, *Christianity in Africa*, 2.

questions that are often ignored."[8] Urban youth today often do not appreciate their traditions and heritage because these traditions have not been passed on to them accurately. But their Christian identity today includes understanding the origins of Christianity in Africa and appreciating the significance of their African traditions in their ongoing faith journey. It is against this background that we reflect on what African spirituality is and how its links to tradition influences being a Christian today.

Role of Traditional Culture in Developing a Christian Identity

This chapter assumes that misconceptions about African spirituality are linked to misconceptions about when Christianity was birthed on this continent. In a postmodern consumerist culture, youth often struggle to identify with their traditional heritage. It is assumed that this tension stems from misconceptions about the value of traditional culture in shaping who we are today, including our Christian identity.

Tradition

Just as there are contested accounts of African Christianity, opinions on the value and place of tradition also vary. Some believe that African traditions have endured despite colonial empires and the type of Christianity they advocated,[9] while others believe that this is a stereotypical view of tradition.[10] The latter view recognizes that traditions become diluted as they are passed on from one generation to the next. The former view laments the fact that despite strong traditions in some cultural contexts, urban youth today tend to be indifferent to traditional values. This is evident in their lack of respect for elders and their disconnection from extended family. What these youth do not realize is that where they come from (their traditions) is tied to who they are today (their identity). Christian youth ministry that is committed to a Christian theology rooted in Africa should aim to revive those traditional practices that, although condemned by missionaries, are true to Scripture. It is challenging to discern which aspects of traditional culture are biblical and which not. Being "biblical"

---

8. Michael, *Christian Theology*, xvi.

9. Toyin, *The power of African cultures*.

10. Lubowa, "Attitudes of Christian missionaries towards African traditional religious beliefs in East Africa during the British colonial rule", 193–199.

requires new contextual readings of the Bible rather than reliance on passed down Western ways of reading it.

African Spirituality

According to Jackson, African people see everything around them as a channel and means of revelation from God.[11] Since God created the universe, this includes God's messages in nature:

> To Africans, God is a living reality and his existence is consciously affirmed in everyday interactions. In prayers, ceremonies, songs, proverbs and moral lessons, Africans generally call upon or make reference to the Supreme Being who controls and directs events in the world. In traditional African sense and setting, there are no atheists, but rather polytheists.[12]

While the supremacy of God is central to African spirituality, he is perceived as being assisted by spirits, shrines, and gods. Shrines serve as a medium for facilitating communication between gods and humans, similar to the role of priests during the Old Testament period. Priests and gods perform religious rituals on behalf of communities, with water gods playing significant roles in healing and traditional medicine. For example, the water goddess "Nne Mmiri" of the Igbo people in Nigeria is visited by people with mental illnesses and gynaecological problems.[13] God is also experienced through natural elements such as the sun, stars, lightning, and life itself. Spirits serve as messengers of the Supreme Being.[14] These spirits – who can be either good or bad – have distinctive personalities, extraordinary powers, and can intervene at will. They serve in mediatory roles and are not subject to human limitations. Finally, one cannot discuss African spirituality without acknowledging the role of ancestors. For certain African tribes,

> life is a cycle that moves from birth to death and, passing through the spiritual or ancestral world, comes back to reincarnating birth – a worldview that culminates in the ancestral belief that death is only a transition from the human plane to the spirit/ ancestral world . . . while the people believe in the Supreme Being,

---

11. Jackson, "Spirituality of Wisdom," 154–55.
12. Michael, *Christian Theology*, 64.
13. Motty, *Indigenous Christian Disciple-Making*, xxi, 133.
14. Motty, 93–95.

they look up to the ancestors for life's practical needs. Every child is initiated into the soul covenant relationship with the ancestral world.[15]

This has implications for how the gospel is explained, internalized, and lived out. It also plays a crucial role in how we explain who Jesus Christ is, which will be discussed later in this chapter.

African spirituality is about placing life into perspective and focusing on wholeness and community. This community serves as a source of wisdom for future generations. Olupona says that the term "spirituality" is not found in a number of traditions; instead, each tradition has to clarify its own understanding of this concept.[16] Unfortunately, the slave trade has resulted in many Africans not being able to connect with their traditions. According to Olupona, many African people today, especially elders, view their classical religious heritage with nostalgia for a paradise lost because they responded to conquest with fierce resistance and, in most cases, adopted the new spirituality by integrating it with their own traditions to create a distinct African expression of spirituality.[17] One of the core challenges in understanding African spirituality today is the lack of recognition by scholars of those who practice these traditions, leading to widespread misunderstanding about these traditions.[18] Another challenge is that churches have not taken seriously the significance of African spirituality when discipling young people:

> Churches in Africa face two choices: either tread the path of indifference to Africa's orientation and aspiration or respect and identify with the African spiritual reality . . . the mainline (mission) churches that hold tenaciously to western orientation and interpretation would rather uphold theology for its own sake, and so they are fated to be on the margin of the religious life of Africa (which requires a form of) spiritual decolonization.[19]

In African spirituality, God is viewed as a more perfect being rather than as an impersonal force that separates the divine from humans.[20] This worldview

---

15. Ephirim-Donkor, *African Spirituality: On becoming ancestors*, 37.

16. Olupona, *African Spirituality*, xii.

17. Olupona, xv.

18. Olupona, xxviii. It is important to note that I, too, serve as an academic scholar outside of the Black traditions of African spirituality. I aim to represent the perspectives of these views as accurately as I can.

19. Olupona, xxix.

20. Michael, *Christian Theology*, 64.

does not place God as the only Lord of a person's life but places him alongside other deities. Before passing judgement, we should ask ourselves whether we sometimes place our possessions, position, or careers alongside God.

African spirituality prioritizes the notion of communal rather than individual personhood. In modernity, however, individualism is the dominant principle that determines social ordering, and almost everything is understood in terms of how well or ill it serves the individual. In the African view, it is the community that defines the person as a person, and this status can only be attained by fulfilling certain community expectations. These expectations consist of obligations, responsibilities, norms, and achievements that are recognized by the community as pertinent to the concept of personhood. Failure to fulfil these communal obligations can lead to the loss of personhood.[21] Chifeche and Motty both argue that while individuals should be understood within their cultural context, they should not be defined by culture. [22] Young people should be encouraged to examine, question, and seek feedback about their own behaviour. This should be embraced in a legacy of oral history on this continent. If this is not encouraged, youth may begin to develop their own belief systems based on their urban contexts, which may result in alienation from their tribal or cultural heritage.

An important aspect of African spirituality is the perception of time. Africans view time as an event and refuse to rush into the future! Their belief that no condition is permanent allows them to face life with patience, endurance, and perseverance. This perspective is critical for youth in busy urban contexts because it encourages the Christian values of perseverance and learning through trials. Understanding and respecting time in this way helps to intentionally promote and develop a culture of sharing because faith formation depends greatly on the gift of creating time to be with one another – time to hear and respond to one another's stories, both positive and negative, or to simply be a non-anxious caring presence.[23]

Urban Youth Identity

An African identity is not limited to the external factors related to tradition; rather, it is an inherited worldview. Many young Africans do not realize that they are born with certain intuitions and premonitions related to this world-

---

21. Táíwò, Unpublished public lecture.
22. Chifeche, "Youth Ministry," 93; Motty, *Indigenous Christian Disciple-Making*, 74.
23. Wimberly and Parker, "In Search of Wisdom," 19.

view, which influences how they think, believe, and live.[24] When this cultural heritage is not taken seriously, youth find themselves torn between the teachings of modern churches and the expectations of their familial traditions. One example of this would be a contestation between following the traditions of ancestors or of Christ which results in a dual allegiance. Urban youth may claim that Western cultures are more relevant to issues they face today, arguing against the notion of a purely African identity. This could lead to a conflict between following ancestral traditions and following Christ, resulting in a dual allegiance What is the essence of what it means to be African in a globalized world? The challenge for youth ministry is to help these young people in developing a transformed African worldview that is rooted in their relationship with Jesus Christ and based on sound contextual readings of the Bible. This demands that youth ministry pay greater attention to Christian apologetics, teaching young people the history of the Bible, how it came to us, and how to interpret it for themselves.

According to Taiwo,

> In traditional society, the tribe is the authority that defines what is right or wrong. It is the custodian of traditions, values and beliefs. It helps the education, assimilation and incorporation of the newly born African child. It also provides the individual with ethnic pride, determines his taste, fashion, aesthetics, language, and other cultural predilections . . . African society generally believed that it is in our "doing" of the accepted norms or obligations of the society that we attain a certain degree of personhood. This is outside the sphere of "being" and annihilates the individuality of the persons for the sake of communal solidarity. This makes it impossible to deal with human beings apart from their culture or identity.[25]

Youth in urban communities are frequently driven by capitalistic agendas that emphasize personal success and identity. Achievements are seen as the result of one's own hard work, while failure is attributed to poor personal performance, which is a problematic view, especially since youth unemployment levels are high in many African cities. Traditional African communities are complex; while young people are not recognized as full persons until they conform to communal rules, yet they also need their communities to support them

---

24. Important to note is that different African tribes view and express this differently. Some of these differences are informed by theologies held.

25. Táíwò, Unpublished public lecture.

in this process. The traditional concept of family includes not only the married couple and their offspring but also other generations, including departed relatives and the unborn. Family systems are thus mixed, transgenerational, and highly inclusive. Children are considered good news and viewed as signs of security and blessing, with the birth of a child being seen as evidence of a fruitful marriage. The birth of a child is also regarded as a communal event, and the child is named according to family customs. Sometimes, the father or mother or even a relative may give the child a name, and this name is one that means something to the family and to the future of the child. Names are given purposefully to reflect both the past and future of the child.[26]

Another example of the complexity of traditional African communities is the expectation concerning traditional rites of passage related to circumcision and marriage. Respect within the community depends on adhering to these traditions. Marriage is important to traditional communities because it sustains the legacy of these tribal groups. In traditional African communities, marriage is between a male and a female, with parents choosing whom their children will marry.[27] Postmodern urban youth are challenging these traditional notions of marriage. Many African states now acknowledge different sexualities and advocate for same-sex marriage. This challenges the young person's identity and place within their community. Given that life is not permanent, the concept of "kairos" – an understanding of time that recognizes significant points in our lives when we awaken to and respond to the call of God – is important, particularly in today's busy, individualistic, and competitive society, where families often do not eat together, neighbours do not know one another, and the struggle for economic sufficiency and gain prevails. We must recognize and affirm our interconnectedness by creating environments where hospitality, healing, and wholeness flourish.

Implications for Christian Youth Today
Christian Spirituality and the Challenges Youth Face

This section describes Christian spirituality and explains how it differs from the core elements of traditional African spirituality. The aim is to help young people embrace a Christian spirituality that is distinctly African. Like African spirituality, Christianity also places a high value on community. It is within the faith community that young people learn from other Christians – both young

---

26. Motty, *Indigenous Christian Disciple-Making*, 147–57.
27. Motty, 141–42.

and old – experience life together and engage in activities that help them to grow in their faith. The distinction lies in the relationship this community has with Jesus Christ and the Holy Spirit. What unifies this community is the belief in Jesus Christ's death, burial, and resurrection for our sins. Beyond this belief is a lifestyle of obedience to him and his word by intentionally responding to what he has done. Those who belong to this community choose to place Christ above all other deities. When faced with trials and suffering, they do not resort to witchcraft but rely on this Triune God, learning how to do so from this faith community. African Christians must be pointed back to the mighty power of Jesus and his ability to protect believers from the powers of witchcraft and evil spirits.[28] The Bible teaches that human beings are created in the image and likeness of God. This means that young people, as human beings, are closely connected to God and not just to the human community. As human beings, our personhood derives from God.[29]

The challenge, however, is that much of our theology is separated from the realities of our faith journey. The spiritual beings mentioned earlier evoke fear among many Africans. African Christians are called to act in the same authority that Jesus exercised during his earthly ministry. This would place them above the forces of witchcraft, evil spirits, and other spiritual forces that have continually troubled and oppressed the African people.[30] They need to be taught and to experience that victory over such fears comes from resting in Christ. Reliance on the truths of Scripture protects Christians from a life that is controlled by these spiritual beings and encourages a life that acknowledges the sovereignty of our Supreme God and understands that these traditional spirits are secondary to God's power and presence in our lives. According to Jackson,[31] the traditional African worldview tends to exaggerate the powers and activities of these fallen spirits.

George describes six things that should inform our Christian worldview and faith:

- Spirituality is about the whole person and encompasses all that God has made us to be. This perspective rejects any dualistic views about how we are to live.
- Spiritual theology centers on the Trinitarian God of love and grace, expressed through relationship, community, and love.

---

28. Jackson, "Spirituality of Wisdom," 98.
29. Táíwò, Unpublished public lecture.
30. Jackson, "Spirituality of Wisdom," 99.
31. Jackson, 100.

- In the journey of faith, spirituality is sustained by means of grace. A core teaching of the Christian faith that youth must grasp is that God is gracious and that we are who we are because of his grace. The many expectations and challenges faced by youth living in busy cities and attending busy schools and churches results in their feeling as if they need to earn God's approval by meeting expectations rather than being who they are called to be. This is one key reason youth may focus more on works than on cultivating a close relationship with God.

- Christian spirituality is about a journey from achievement to rest, building a life that does not only do and go but prioritizes being and listening.

- The hard reality of being a Christian includes embracing suffering and conflict as part of our faith journey, and this is another theological truth that youth must accept.

- We are not alone in this journey because we are part of the priesthood of all believers, called to live lives that reflect the character of Christ, the spirit of Christian unity, our wider Christian heritage, and true ecumenism. Youth need to understand that their commitment to the faith community is not merely for what they can get out of this but also about growing and learning together. Young people should also be exposed to the faith traditions of other churches and not be isolated because of fear of losing them.[32]

African Spirituality and Salvation

There is a significant difference between the biblical understanding of salvation and the African perspective. According to Taiwo, almost every religious practice among the African people – including rituals, festivities, sacrifices, exorcisms, and divination – stems from a deep desire to attain some form of salvation or deliverance from the social, spiritual, and existential problems of their world.[33] Many Africans are born into conditions of poverty, illness, famine, and lack of basic necessities, which causes them to view salvation primarily in physical and material terms, rather than in spiritual terms. This results in a drive towards a "doing" rather than a "being" spirituality, focusing on the pursuit of physical well-being in the present world. This is why they

---

32. George, *For All the Saints*, 5–7.
33. Táíwò, Unpublished public lecture.

believe that existential challenges in their lives require the help and presence of divinities and gods to mediate between them and God. This could also explain why certain forms of Pentecostalism that preach a materialistic concept of salvation are flourishing on the continent.

Africans often do not teach or adhere to the biblical teaching about the fall of humanity. The absence of this concept in traditional African religions naturally makes it difficult to communicate the biblical teaching of salvation because, in Christian thought, it is the fall that necessitates salvation. Thus, since this concept of the fall is absent in traditional African religion, salvation in terms of redemption of the soul is also largely absent.[34] African Christianity emphasizes the centrality of the spiritual dimension of salvation, where forgiveness of sins is found exclusively in the atoning sacrifice of Jesus Christ. It is also important that the doctrines of justification and sanctification are taught and contextualized. African Christians hold to being justified by faith in Christ and continually formed into who he has called us to be, and it is this understanding that motivates them to forsake those elements of their traditions that do not align with the word of God. Taiwo writes,

> In traditional society, sanctification takes the form of "holy baths" and other ritualistic observances . . . when the client is conceived as unclean, the priest advises a certain cleansing ritual. The client does everything commanded by the priest in order to achieve the ritualistic cleanness desired by the oracles. The Bible teaches the progressive work of God and man which aims to make us more conformed to the image of Christ and less compatible to the ways of sin.[35]

Salvation, then, is not dependent on the individual or on the priest as a mediator. African traditional religion lacks the notion of original sin and redemption. Unlike Western Christianity, which has a linear conception of time, African traditions are cyclical, repetitive, and lack the notion of eternity. However, they are not entirely devoid of the notion of redemption and salvation. Olupona says,

> Christ through the agency of his resurrection and ascension becomes the supreme ancestor who went to the realm of the ancestor spirits and gods and thus became endowed with power and authority that transcends those of the ancestor . . . the implica-

---

34. Taiwo, 168–70.
35. Taiwo, 180–84.

tion of such understanding of Jesus is that it assumes authority that He supersedes those of the ancestors. Jesus now perceived as Lord of both the living, the dead and the ancestor, successfully displaces the mediatorial function of our natural "spirit fathers" and assumes such roles in very important redefined forms that transcend those of the ancestors.[36]

Christian Theology of Youth Ministry

One of the challenges faced by youth ministries is that they are often based on thematic programmes rather than a sound theological foundation. Many youth workers believe that what is important is having good programmes that attract large numbers. However, many testify to burnout, running out of ideas, and lacking energy to follow through with these initiatives. Bearing in mind the complexities discussed in this chapter and the importance of faith formation for African youth, it is imperative that our approach to youth ministry is based on relevant and contextual Christian theology.

We recognize that our understanding of Christianity may be shaped by how strongly we are aligned with traditional African norms. This section calls for a theology that takes seriously the context and language of the youth we minister to. It focuses on the centrality of the Bible in Christian theology, addressing the importance of contextual relevance and the languages in which it is communicated.

Importance of context

At the beginning of this chapter, I briefly discussed the disputes surrounding the timing and manner in which Christianity found its way to Africa. Many Africans, from their standpoint as a marginalized voice in the history of our continent, argue that foreign missionaries did not contextualize the Bible, by which they mean that the biblical story was not adapted to address the spirituality and needs of African people. As already noted, some Christian missionaries influenced Africans to live according to their own interpretations of the Bible.

In discussing the need for a Christian theology that takes African traditions seriously, Matthew Michael says that the Bible must engage in a close dialogue with African traditions because "Christian theology cannot afford to isolate itself from the daily existential challenges" of African people, par-

---

36. Olupona, *African Spirituality*, 136.

ticularly young people.[37] "Any theology that ignores the human context and its myriad problems has isolated God from the human context."[38] He adds that theology must be based on the authoritative canon of the Christian Scriptures and not on the conflicting contextual realities. Whatever the challenges of our context, theology must seek to come to terms with the contemporary trends or challenges as expressed and experienced in popular myths, religious beliefs, and political ideologies of the time. There is no perfect theology that fits all contextual realities of all people. While most theologies seek to be universal in their relevance to the entire globe, fundamentally, theology involves the reflections of human beings in their various contexts on the divine being.[39] Jurgens agrees that religion is a deep-rooted aspect of Africa's cultural life, shaping the life experiences of millions of Africans and steering them towards an approach to religion that is deep, fervent, and at once personal and social.[40]

The importance of language

Just as we have emphasized the need to contextualize the truth of the Bible, Bediako argues that it should also be translated into the native languages of the people.[41] He adds that Africa needs Christianity – but a Christianity free from European distortions. Failure to share the Christian message in a language that Africans understood has contributed to the African identity problem. Language – both verbal and non-verbal – plays a key role in shaping identity and empowering the values of a people group. Parker says that oral tradition has been essential for Africans in surviving the dehumanizing experiences of slavery and in preserving a valued identity wherever they found themselves.[42] She adds that text-based Christian education only became prominent in Black churches in the twentieth century. Today, much of the theological activity in Christian Africa takes the form of oral theology based on the lived experiences of Christians.[43] However, this approach is not always appreciated because it has not been formally recorded. The African shape that Christianity is taking following its translation into African languages and cultural forms has resulted

---

37. Michael, *Christian Theology*, 17–18.
38. Michael, xv.
39. Michael, 22.
40. Jurgens, *Africa in Fact*, 81.
41. Bediako, *Christianity in Africa*, 11–14.
42. Parker, 58.
43. Bediako, *Christianity in Africa*, 33.

in the development of Christian life and thought through interaction with African cultures and traditions.[44]

Perhaps the real challenge of giving primacy to the word of God is that African theology will have to make a deliberate attempt to relate theological reflection and construction to the actual vernacular articulation of faith within the African Christian experience. Taking the vernacular seriously is not merely a cultural exercise but a theological necessity. African theology's methods, interests, and goals will then be shaped and controlled by the genuine needs of Christianity in African life. It will also be in a stronger position to demonstrate the ecumenical significance of the African experience. Thus, African theology will fulfil a crucial pastoral function – namely, nurturing and equipping a people of God who have heard about the wonders of God in their own languages.[45]

Biblical Practices to Enhance the Christian Spirituality of African Youth

It is important to give young people biblical alternatives to navigate the challenges they face as Christians. The following points, while not exhaustive, have been chosen because they connect important aspects of being an African with the biblical call of Christians. The hope is that as these youth grow in their faith they will gain a fuller understanding of their African Christian identity. Young people should be encouraged to do the following:[46]

- Be intentional about growing in your relationship with God because growing spiritually is all about the way we encounter and experience God, the transformation of our consciousness, and the internalization of our faith.
- Commit to a church (faith community) that is grounded in solid theology. Youth should be encouraged to engage and grapple with God's word in an environment in which other generations offer support and guidance. However, Taiwo cautions that strong tribal ties may enter the church with terrible consequences.[47] People's commitment to tribal interests can take priority over their commitment to the Christian faith. The call is not merely to join a church and

---

44. Corrigan and Dutton, *Fulfilling the Great Commission*, 78.
45. Bediako, *Christianity in Africa*, 72–73.
46. McGrath, "Loving God," 13–23; Williams, "C. S. Lewis," 180–92.
47. Táíwò, Unpublished public lecture.

become a nominal Christian but to contribute to this community and learn from it.

- Avoid intellectualizing your faith. Consumerism lends itself to the serious danger of an arid evangelical rationalism that erodes the God-given appeal of the gospel to our hearts, imaginations, and emotions by demanding that we limit our knowledge of God to the mind. Faith should be intellectual, affective, and active.[48]

- Christian spirituality is grounded in the awareness of being a condemned sinner who has been utterly transformed by divine forgiveness. There are people in "Christian" settings who believe in Jesus but not in God.[49] Spirituality is a matter of living our lives in the reality of God, and this is supernatural because obedience to Christ is a supernatural act that cannot be accomplished except in the power of a "life from above."

- Superficiality is the curse of our age; young people need the support of authentic and mature Christians.

- The centrality of God's word requires listening to God's words, reflecting on them, and rehearsing God's deeds. Memorizing Scripture is fundamental in faith formation.

- Commit to prayer and fasting because God reveals himself to us through these practices. Prayer lists can be helpful, and fasting can be a way to assert our will against appetites or distractions like watching television or reading popular magazines so that we can focus on what God is doing and saying.

- Commit to reading and studying Christian books on relevant topics. Doing this in groups of twos or threes can provide accountability and invite different perspectives. This approach could also be applied to reading God's word.

Conclusion

While there is much to learn about African spirituality, this chapter has focused on how to help Christian young people living in African cities to relate to but also be aware of differences between African spirituality and an authentic relationship with Christ. African youth need to be taught about both their African

---

48. Strommen and Hardel, *Passing On the Faith*.
49. Willard, "Spiritual Formation," 42–44.

heritage and biblical truths of what it means to follow Christ. As Oosthuizen notes,

> The contemporary task to African philosophy and African theology should be to reconstruct African value systems but the collapse of values in the urban area cannot be restored merely by economic means and methods. It is here that the church has a task, but the mainline churches especially have lost contact with the grass-roots situation. The African theologian should examine the fundamental principles that stimulate traditional religion; look at the foreign influences and the conflicts to which these give rise; examine issues such as inter-human relationships, fellowship, healing in its holistic context, church liturgy, and spontaneous religious expression such as composition of hymns and so on. African cultural life has also changed and can never be the same again, certain demands of modern society cannot be met in the traditional context, especially on the scientific and industrial level.[50]

African youth need the guidance of the Christian community to grow in their faith amid a consumeristic culture that challenges traditional values. This guidance should take into consideration the traditional underpinnings of African spirituality, the contemporary issues these youth face, and the contextual application of biblical truths.

Discussion Questions

1. Why is it important to discuss the history of Christianity from an African perspective in relation to youth and spirituality?

2. What does African spirituality encompass?

3. Compare and contrast biblical spirituality and African spirituality.

4. Why do we need a Christian theology of youth ministry?

5. What is the significance of context and language in a Christian theology of youth ministry?

6. What are some biblical practices that strengthen the Christian spirituality of African youth?

---

50. Oosthuizen, "African Traditional Religion," 278.

Bibliography

Bediako, Kwame. *Christianity in Africa: The Renewal of a Non-Western Religion*. Edinburgh: Edinburgh University Press; Maryknoll: Orbis Books, 1995.

Chifeche, Victoria Armando. "Youth Ministry in Mozambique: A Practical Theological Evaluation." PhD thesis, University of Pretoria, 2018.

Ephirim-Donkor, Anthony. *African Spirituality: On becoming ancestors*. Lanham: Hamilton Books, 2021.

Falola, Toyin. *The Power of African Cultures*. University of Rochester Press, 2003.

George, Timothy, and Alister McGrath, eds. *For All the Saints: Evangelical Theology and Christian Spirituality*. Louisville: Westminster John Knox, 2003.

Hassan, Tugume Lubowa. "Attitudes of Christian missionaries towards African traditional religious beliefs in East Africa during the British colonial rule." *African Journal of History and Culture* 7, no. 10 (2015): 193–99.

Jackson, Jonathan, Jr. "Forming a Spirituality of Wisdom." In *Search of Wisdom: Faith Formation in the Black Church*, edited by Anne E. Streaty Wimberly and Evelyn L. Parker, 154–66. Nashville: Abingdon, 2002.

Mawuko-Yevugah, L. C., and P. Ugor, eds. *African Youth Cultures in a Globalized World: Challenges, Agency and Resistance*. New York: Ashgate, 2015.

McGrath, Alister. "Loving God with Heart and Mind: The Theological Foundations of Spirituality." In *For All the Saints*, edited by Timothy George and Alister McGrath, 11–26. Louisville: Westminster John Knox, 2003.

Michael, Matthew. *Christian Theology and African Traditions*. Eugene: Wipf & Stock, 2013.

Motty, Bauta D. *Indigenous Christian Disciple-Making*. Nigeria: ECWA Productions, 2013.

Olupona, Jacob K. *African Spirituality: Forms, Meanings, and Expressions*. New York: Crossroad, 2000.

Oosthuizen, Gerhardus Cornelis. "The Task of African Traditional Religion in the Church's Dilemma in South Africa." *African Spirituality* (2000): 277–83.

Strommen, Merton P., and Richard A. Hardel. *Passing On the Faith: A Radical New Model for Youth and Family Ministry*. Winona: St. Mary's Press, 2000.

Táíwò, Olúfẹ́mi. Unpublished public lecture. Presented at the Department of Language, Linguistics and Philosophy, University of the West Indies, Mona, May 15, 2009. 1–10.

Willard, Dallas. "Spiritual Formation in Christ Is for the Whole Life and the Whole Person." In *For All the Saints*, edited by Timothy George and Alister McGrath, 39–53. Louisville: Westminster John Knox, 2003.

Williams, Wallace A. "C. S. Lewis: Spiritual Disciplines for Mere Christians." In *For All the Saints*, edited by Timothy George and Alister McGrath, 177–94. Louisville: Westminster John Knox, 2003.

Wimberly, Anne E. Streaty, and Evelyn L. Parker, eds. *In Search of Wisdom: Faith Formation in the Black Church*. Nashville: Abingdon, 2002.

4

Youth, Work, and Community Development

Cavens Kithinji

Introduction

Africa is said to have the highest concentration of young people in the world. According to United Nations statistics from 2015, nearly 20 percent of Africa's population is youth, and it is projected that by 2030, Africa's youth population will account for about 42 percent of the world's youth population. By 2100, Africa's youth is expected to grow by 181.4 percent.[1] While this means that Africa will have high production potential, early action must be taken to harness this potential. If the youth population is not engaged in meaningful and productive work, this could lead to an increased youth dependency ratio, further hindering economic development, which was only around 3.7 percent in African countries in 2019. The demographic dividend in Africa will be realized if the youth dependency ratio decreases.[2] Therefore, it is essential to engage youth in matters related to all aspects of development: social (family, community, religious, cultural), political, and economic.

Youth play a key role in community development. Therefore, we must identify what the community and the church can do to guide and direct them towards meaningful engagement in work. Although the idea that youth are generally rebellious has been prevalent in research for some time, the rise of Positive Youth Development (PYD) discourse suggests that youth, despite being problematic at times, can discover their life purpose and develop posi-

---

1. Rocca and Schultes, *Africa's Youth*, 1.
2. Bloom, "Africa's Prospects," 13.

tive work attitudes if they receive proper guidance, thereby becoming major positive contributors to community growth.[3] We must ask the right questions: How can the church engage youth in ways that foster the right attitudes towards work? What activities can we develop to facilitate this learning process and bring about the desired change?

The Change That Must Be

The dynamism of youth behaviour, the lack of understanding of this sector of the population, and the general lack of employment opportunities is one of the reasons leading to formation of gangs among young people. Being part of these gangs and with no income makes them easy targets to be used in political violence by politicians. This has led to a sense of disillusionment among communities and negative labelling of youth. These social and economic challenges prevent youth from realizing their potential, resulting in feelings of being sidelined or pushed towards what is considered the secondary sector of the economy – for instance, music, dance, and art – where they struggle to make ends meet.[4]

We must acknowledge that everyone has natural talent and creativity, which are assets that the church must harness to bring about necessary change in society. Unless we recognize the potential in this important segment of our population and reverse this unhelpful trend, we risk this group becoming a burden to society. As the population increases and job opportunities decrease, the church must create avenues that encourage and nurture innovation and new ideas.

The church has a vital role to play in ensuring the economic well-being of this very important segment of our population. In this regard, the church needs to engage youth in strategies that positively influence them as they seek to navigate the world of work, offer guidance, and seek to create work opportunities. It is also important to recognize that change often takes time and that it must be intentional, which means that the church must give thought to and plan for the desired change.

---

3. Méndez, "Positive Youth Development," 76.
4. Kilonzo, "Youth, Religion, and Development," 103.

Positive Youth Development and Work

The Positive Youth Development (PYD) perspective explores the argument that human potential for systematic change in behaviour exists as a result of mutually influential relationships between youth and their families, communities, cultures (including the church), and the environment.[5] The primary organizing principle of PYD is to provide avenues through which youth can access positive experiences, resources, and opportunities for developmental outcomes that are beneficial for both themselves and society.[6]

In shaping youth perspectives on development, the church and other faith-based organizations will seek to incorporate spirituality. Spirituality is crucial for developing a positive sense of self and identity that enables youth to identify and pursue their life paths.[7] Lerner et al. conclude that if young people have mutually beneficial relationships with the people and institutions in society, they are likely to develop ideologies that make them positive contributors to themselves, as well as to their families, communities, and society.[8]

Benson et al. conclude from the literature that the principles in the PYD field include the following:

> (1) All youth have the inherent capacity for positive growth and development; (2) A positive developmental trajectory is enabled when youth are embedded in relationships, contexts, and ecologies that nurture their development; (3) The promotion of positive development is further enabled when youth participate in multiple, nutrient rich relationships, contexts, and ecologies; (4) All youth benefit from these relationships, contexts, and ecologies . . .; (5) Community is a viable and critical "delivery system" for positive youth development; (6) Youth are major actors in their own development and are significant (and underutilized) resources for creating the kinds of relationships, contexts, ecologies, and communities that enable positive youth development.[9]

In reflection of these principles, the outlook of the church should be reflective of the belief that God created certain abilities and positivity in every single person. It is the responsibility of the church to nurture this potential and ensure

---

5. Lerner et al., "Positive Youth Development," 20.
6. Benson and Scales, "Positive Youth Development," 218.
7. Lerner et al., "On Making Humans Human."
8. Lerner et al., "Positive Youth Development: Processes Programs, and Problematics," 47.
9. Benson and Scales, "Positive Youth Development," 218.

that it germinates and grows. Churches can build intentional relationships and environments that foster positive growth through sustainable programmes designed for this purpose. The church community creates a system that is conducive for the positive learning of work values. In such an environment, inviting youth to participate in implementing programmes creates a sense of ownership and places the responsibility for success in their own hands. In PYD theory, concepts such as Competence, Confidence, Connection, Character, Caring, and Contribution are foundational for teaching values essential to work, and research shows that these concepts have led to positive youth development.

The church's role in facilitating change among youth cannot be overemphasized. Following the principles mentioned above, together with biblical guidance, the church as a community should create a system that addresses moral issues, work, commitment, and life purpose. This requires church leadership to be more intentional in structuring youth programmes that have clearly defined outcome goals. Such programmes help to form both character and a positive social outlook. The church must consider these questions: Are we placing too much emphasis on programmes for mature church members at the expense of youth? How much is the church investing in developing the skills of the youth workers on its staff? To what extent is the church preparing young people for the workplace by investing in youth programmes that focus on skills development and instilling positive work values?

Motivation for Involvement in Youth Development and Work

The recognition that youth should actively contribute to the positive growth of the community is the primary motivation for involvement in youth development work. For young people, this motivation may arise from a variety of factors such as fulfilling a school requirement, improving their chances of getting into college or securing a desirable job, building networks, enhancing existing skills, earning money, or simply spending time with friends. It is important to leverage these motivations to help young people improve their skills, talents, and abilities, thereby enhancing their intellectual, physical, and emotional capabilities to express their concerns about issues and improve their quality of life.[10] Whatever the motivation, getting young people involved is the starting point for shaping their perspectives and perhaps changing their orientation. Motivation is the soil for planting ideas about the virtues of work. It

---

10. Glatzer, Camfield, Møller, and Rojas, *Global Handbook*, 814.

is important to clearly articulate the benefits of such programmes in a manner that creates and sustains interest among youth. Creative youth workers are needed to design interactions that engage young people and promote a sense of self-actualization among them.

The church's very existence depends on how well it develops the youth – both spiritually and in their engagement with work. Self-fulfilment in life comes from accomplishing one's purpose. A church that invests in helping its young members find this fulfilment will secure its own future because there is a sense of belonging and commitment to the church even if individuals move away from the community.

The church has a mandate to foster leadership within the community and the country. I believe that leadership and work values are best taught in a church setting, which benefits not only the church but also families, communities, and humanity. Therefore, shaping the orientation of youth should be a primary concern of the church, especially because values instilled during the formative years are often solidified during this stage of their lives.

According to George and Uyanga, youths are major determinants of the level of development in any society. Without youths, there can be no sustenance of society as no society can be self-sustaining without its human components of which the major workforce is the youths.[11] It is important to harness this energy and turn it into a development force for the community. The prosperity of a community depends on the positive engagement of members from all segments of its population.

To view youth solely as dependants is to exclude them from efforts to create a community that benefits from all its members, which is also detrimental to their own growth. London, Zimmerman, and Erbstein argue that isolating youth from community and organizational development stunts their ability to cultivate personal growth, engage in communities, and effect institutional and community change.[12] Throughout the ages, in every society, youths have been key determinants of development. These arguments present the premise for engaging the youth as the primary workforce in any society. Developing their skills and shaping their attitude towards work would thus make sense for the church.

---

11. George and Uyanga, "Youth and Moral Values," 43.
12. London, Zimmerman, and Erbstein, "Youth-Led Research," 34.

Equipping Youth for Work in the Community

The potential of youth in African communities remains largely untapped. Changing this situation requires intentional and well-thought-out strategies. The goal is to formulate a system that gives the church a roadmap for engagement with youth, particularly during the brief school holiday periods. An analysis of the most successful community-scale initiatives reveals three key principles that are critical to the success of any youth empowerment programme.[13]

The first principle involves asking the right strategic questions in the right order: What do you desire to see changed among youth in respect to work? What is the time frame required to achieve this change? What resources are needed and what resources are available? How best can this change be achieved? What lessons can we learn from others? Reflecting on such questions will help in planning within the church's limitations and identifying potential resources that can be obtained both internally and from external partners.

The second principle focuses on creating organizational structures and processes that involve youth and adults in joint decision-making and action. This approach is important because it encourages youth to take ownership of the process and promotes a role-modelling effect as the two groups work together in this programme. The key elements necessary for success include the church's flexibility in accommodating such programmes, support from the leadership, working within a time frame, an effective feedback system, and openness to new ideas. Given that the African population has a median age of 19.7, it is important to include youth – who make up the majority of the population – in meaningful work and leadership roles. Since young people are at a stage in life when they are developing mentally, it is essential to pass on the ideals necessary for work and community leadership during this time. This concept of community resonates strongly with sociological definitions that emphasize locality, structural components, and personal bonds that derive from a shared territory.[14]

The third principle, focuses on marshalling resources critical for implementing the strategy. The importance of inclusivity is highlighted in this to ensure every member of the society (including the youth) contribute to the implementation of the development strategies. It is also important to analyse the church's capacity to influence, including that of the youthful members. The skills identified in the first principle may be inherent among youth. Since peer

---

13. Campbell and Erbstein, "Engaging Youth," 72–88.

14. Brennan and Barnett, "Bridging Community," 306.

influence plays a major role among youth, this capacity to influence should be harnessed positively. Therefore, participation is important, and the programme designed should also seek the participation of other church members and leaders with diverse skills and extensive networks. Brennan and Barnett argue that developing youth has a broader impact in the larger community, which includes their neighbourhoods, schools, and significant relationships.[15] This also creates networks and provides opportunities for youth to participate and engage positively in work.

Church Work Model for Youth

While acknowledging that there are interesting youth work models in the literature such as the analysis done by Cooper[16] – a church work model of youth, which incorporates the influence of the church, represents the ideal way to engage youth in teaching, training, and work development, and related attitudes. This aligns with the Social Education Repertoire (SER) model of Butters and Newell as cited in Cooper[17] and the movement-based youth work philosophy formulated by Smith.[18] The model presented in this chapter can be used to develop a customized framework to enable youth to learn and model sustainable work values. Such a model will integrate the principles discussed in the previous section with insights from the book of Daniel in the Bible, providing a framework that churches can use to develop training manuals to guide discussions on youth self-improvement and work.

We first encounter Daniel (also known as Belteshazzar) in an assimilation programme in Babylon after he and several other youth were taken captive from Judah. Little is said about Daniel's life in Judah, although we are told that Daniel and his companions were from "the royal family and the nobility" (Dan 1:3). However, Daniel's interactions with the authorities during the assimilation programme provide insights into who he was and his upbringing as a God-fearing young man.

The first key element of this model is *Spiritual Foundations* (Dan 1:8). Daniel's resolve came from a deep conviction about who he was and his commitment to remaining true to his identity, regardless of the circumstance. This reveals the strength of his beliefs and his upbringing in the faith. While

---

15. Brennan and Barnett, 307.

16. Cooper, "Models of Youth Work."

17. Butters and Newell, *Realities of Training*, 9, in Cooper, 101.

18. Smith, "Youth Work to Youth Development," 46–59.

this resolve is initially presented as personal, it is later depicted as a shared position adopted by Daniel and his friends (Dan 1:11–12). These youth had a strong faith that their request would be granted and that this "meal plan" would work, illustrating that building a strong foundation in God can help to shape right attitudes to work. It is important to design youth programmes that focus on strengthening their spiritual foundations so that they can navigate their work experiences with conviction. As demonstrated by Daniel's story, building the faith of young people will be crucial in how they handle different work situations.

The second key element is *Focus*. It is important to note that Daniel did not concern himself with the Babylonian programme since he did not really have a choice in the matter. Instead, Daniel's focus was God. He understood that he had not left God behind in Judah and that trusting in God was vital in this situation. Although the circumstances were far from ideal, Daniel's focus did not waiver. These youth understood that their survival and success depended on God, and they put this faith into action (Dan 1:12–13), trusting that God had already prepared the way for them – verse 9 tells us that "God had caused the official to show favour and compassion to Daniel."

The third key element is *Training*. The purpose of the assimilation programme for which these young men were selected was to equip them for public service through teaching and training. The selection criteria focused on previous skills, intelligence, being well-informed and knowledgeable persons (Dan 1:4). Having ensured that the candidates possessed these qualities, they were given further training in the language and literature of the Babylonians. Most youth in our churches are a product of school systems that provide skills development and training in various areas, based on a set curriculum. The role of the church is to find ways to enrich these skills and competencies within the school system. In addition, church-based training can be customized to focus on individual interests. There are also tools available that can involve youth, parents, and professionals in the process of determining and enhancing career paths. This does not mean that the church should provide this professional training. However, once career paths are identified, the church can offer programmes that serve as a support system that helps youth to remain focused and provide advice about specialized training. By monitoring young people's progress, the church can foster within youth a sense of care that goes beyond just spiritual considerations. Since work is an important part of a Christian's spiritual growth, it is important that youth understand that God is involved and concerned about their training. As Daniel 1:17 notes, "to these four young men God gave knowledge and understanding of all kinds of literature and learning. And Daniel could understand visions and dreams of all kinds."

After training comes *Evaluation.* Daniel 1:20 describes an evaluation process conducted by the king himself. The results of this evaluation revealed that Daniel and his friends were ten times better than the rest in their cohort. Any programme with clear goals must be evaluated to determine the extent to which these goals have been achieved. Churches must appreciate that after investing resources in youth programmes, it is important to have a clear evaluation process that documents the gains – both intended and unintended – and lessons learned. Such feedback will enable programme designers to make modifications that improve the programme.

As youth move to the workplace, the church could establish a support system to monitor their performance and progress informally by considering questions such as the following: How are youth making progress at their workplace? What values are they demonstrating? How can the church assist? Such a programme is consistent with the idea that Christianity is a lifestyle. We cannot separate work from the church or the church from work since we must live out our Christian values in both settings. Therefore, incorporating this concept in the model fosters a sense of family and community, where members are concerned for one another beyond the church compound.

The final element is *Sustainability.* Throughout the book of Daniel, we read the records of his work successes that spanned the reigns of multiple kings. Alongside this work, we also have records of Daniel's faith and trust in God and his exploits for God. The church's training programmes should aim for sustainable and satisfactory work experiences, where work is not seen as separate from faith in God and young people are encouraged to live out their Christian faith in work settings. While living out one's faith is a personal issue, sustained follow-up and support from the church goes a long way in enhancing this experience. Pastoral care must go beyond church, extending to family settings, community living, and the workplace.

The Model Explained

For the church, a focus on God remains a central element in our engagement with youth. The programme design should clearly emphasize the centrality of God in all activities. In planning such programmes, a key element must be a clear emphasis on enhancing spiritual foundations as the basis on which to establish and build strategies. It is also important to examine church structures to determine where to anchor the programme and to explore how flexible these structures can be in encouraging the participation of key stakeholders, particularly those who are invested in youth. This understanding will enable effective designing and planning of the programme.

After the design and planning stage, the church needs to gather the resources required for implementation. An inclusive approach, where the church takes ownership of the programme and uses its resources and networks to facilitate implementation, would work best. Resource persons should include the target group or those close to the target group. Before training commences, it is important to ensure that the necessary resources are available. The training should be designed based on the needs identified at the planning stage, with a focus on achieving the established goals. If it becomes necessary to revise these goals or activities, such changes should be within the scope of the programme. The programme design should include evaluation, including consideration of what skills have been enhanced, what knowledge has been passed on, and how this can be applied. Having the youth undertake volunteer works at the community level is a good way to make assessment of the programme success.

The programme should be designed to monitor work values such as diligence, integrity, commitment, and service as unto God. In most work environments, performance is measured differently, and those in the programme may not be required to show such outputs. A qualitative tool can be designed to monitor such values. Participants can carry out self-evaluations, followed by peer evaluations using a generalized tool since most participants in the programme may not work in the same organization. In addition, service within the church can also be used to measure some of these values.

It is vital to ensure that the benefits of the programme are sustained over time. A system should be established to provide cohort members with opportunities to work alongside the programme implementers to guide new cohorts through the programme. This will not only reinforce the learning but also give participants a chance to mentor others. This way, the programme becomes sustainable and ensures the sustainability of the values learned. The flow of the model is illustrated in Figure 1.

Guide to the Model Design

The belief that our lives are guided by God and have meaning in God gives believers assurance about two aspects of work: first, that work is a service to both God and humanity, which gives work significance beyond mere financial compensation; and second, that work is fulfilling and progressively guided by God, its author. In this understanding, the church and its members see God as central to any work setting. God is present in our planning and execution of all work activities. This model of work places God at the centre and understands all elements of work in this light.

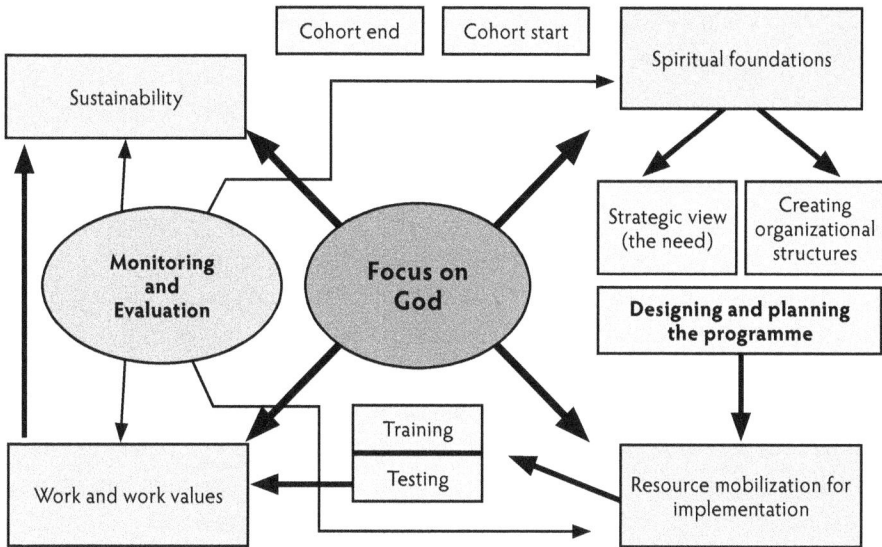

Figure 1: Church Youth Work Model

Spiritual Foundation: In designing this stage, two elements must be upheld: God's purpose in the lives of each individual participant and the purpose of the programme itself. While the programme's purpose can be discerned through prayer, discussion, and planning, each individual's journey to discover their purpose can take longer and can be more difficult to determine. It is important to emphasize that this journey can be shortened if youth are given an opportunity to strengthen their faith in God. The programme should always focus on this aspect by providing opportunities and forums that are designed to help youth to discover their work interests and individual purpose in God. The earlier someone discovers their interest, the better so that they can pursue a more focused career path. It is highly recommended that parents, teachers, and other concerned parties are involved in this process. The following questions can guide the planning of this section to ensure that a strategic approach is adopted:

1. What outcomes are we seeking for our youth in work settings?

2. What is our current position in reference to the outcomes we are seeking in 1. above?

3. What actions will help us to bridge the gap between the current status and the desired outcomes?

4. What indicators will enable us to determine if we have achieved the desired outcomes?

Once these questions have been addressed, we need to carry out an organizational capacity assessment to evaluate the resources available in the church to achieve the desired outcomes. This assessment should also identify any structural concerns that need to be dealt with to ensure the programme's success and establish lines of authority for overseeing the programme.

The questions listed above will help in planning, and specific goals should be established for the programme to address the gaps identified in the desired goals. These goals, which would describe the desired status within the church setting, will be general in nature but precise enough to clarify the desired position. From these goals, planners will formulate objectives – that is, tangible and specific outcomes that are measurable within a specific time frame. Each goal will have one or more objectives that describe the outcomes that will lead to the desired state. The programme's effectiveness will be measured by assessing the achievement of these objectives.

Based on the objectives, a set of activities will be designed. These are specific actions that must be carried out to deliver the expected output or results. Activities will be designed with a timeline for completion and will specify the resources required for implementation as this step is necessary for determining the efficiency of the programme. A clear description of the resources needed – specifying both quality and quantity – will be given. Finally, activity schedules will be determined, specifying when each activity will be carried out and the duration of each, along with an overall timeline for each cohort's programme.

Resources mobilization for implementation: Prior to implementation of the programme, the resources necessary for the activities must be obtained and organized. In order to create a sense of ownership, the entire church, including the participants, should be involved in providing the resources. The results of the capacity assessment exercise carried out in the first phase would be used in the resource mobilization plan, which should be documented based on the specific requirements of each activity designed. As far as possible, it is desirable to involve in the programme church members that naturally have an appeal to the youth or use other church networks to get resource persons. The resource plan will outline when and how much of each resource will be needed, what is currently available, and what will need to be obtained from outside the church.

Using the activity schedule prepared during the planning stage, the implementation phase will commence. It is important that the programme is initially implemented among youth who seem committed to it. Since this programme is designed to continue until participants are established in their roles as workers in various fields, it is advisable to create different cohorts based on their ages and career development stages.

In addition, the programme should also include a system for evaluating the skills attained during implementation. Round-table discussions, with a simple guide on how to direct these conversations, would work well.

Work and Work Values Monitoring: The third element of the model develops a system to monitor how participants apply the work values taught in the programme in the marketplace. This element serves as an internship or practicum, where the church enables participants to put into practice the values taught theoretically. It is important that the church engages participants privately, apart from the performance evaluation systems of the organization where they work. However, obtaining independent feedback from the organization would add value to the individual evaluations, provided that participants consent to such disclosure and the organization's policies permit such an arrangement.

In general, participants should first carry out a self-assessment regarding their performance and work values, followed by a one-on-one session to probe more deeply into their scores. These sessions can be used to affirm their values and share workplace experiences that are relevant to the individual or to the programme. The assessment should start by attempting to gain a general understanding of work schedules, work environments, supervision styles, performance indicators, and general workplace interactions.

Sustainability: In this model, sustainability is designed in two ways. The first is sustainability of the model, meaning that cohorts would be established based on demand. The demand will be created based on the value attached to this training and how well the trainees have sustained the work values gained in the training. The second is the programme design. This design should incorporate a self-sustaining approach, requiring higher investment in terms of time and resources during the first and second phases with reduced investment during the third phase, aiming at independent operation during the fourth phase.

To achieve this, the programme should establish an accountability system among the participants right from the outset. The groups created must be cohesive enough to continue for a number of years despite space limitations. The objective should be for these accountability partners to check on each other and foster an attitude of giving back because they believe in and have experienced the benefits of the programme. These teams should also be involved in the implementation of new cohorts in the future, which will ensure that they are constantly reminded of what they stand for and practice in the marketplace.

Overall, the programme should emphasize facilitation and mentorship. In phase three, programme facilitators will be assigned mentees to work with and will also function as overseers of accountability groups. This will free church youth workers, allowing them to concentrate on new cohorts. It is important to document activities across all phases as evidence of programme continuity.

Regular evaluation of the programme is necessary at all its stages – design, planning, resource mobilization, implementation, a mentorship as they transition to work place, and sustainability – and a monitoring and evaluation system should be integrated into every stage. Plans must be translated into a logical framework that outlines each goal, the corresponding objectives, the activities planned for each objective, and the resources required to carry out the activities. This will help in designing the monitoring and evaluation framework for the programme.

During the planning stage, it is important to establish indicators to measure each element in this logical framework. However, these indicators may be adjusted based on baseline data observed before or during implementation of the programme. The table below documents the requirements of such a system at every stage.

Table 1: Monitoring and evaluation requirements

Logical framework	M&E areas of focus	Elements measured
Goals (strategic view)	Strategic view	Impact (planned and unplanned)
Outcomes (work experience)	Objectives of the programme	Relevance and effectiveness
Outputs (work values)	Learned values as expected from the activities	Effectiveness
Activities (training and testing)	Appropriateness of the activities in light of the resources	Efficiency and quality
Inputs (resources mobilization)	Availability of the resources on time and in the right quantity	Efficiency

The measures used in the above table are explained below:

1. Efficiency will be measured by determining the use of resources and their appropriateness in the light of the activities they are facilitat-

ing and output expected. The element of appropriate use is also captured here.

2. Effectiveness is concerned with the extent to which the programme has achieved the objectives set at the planning stage.

3. Relevance is the measure of validity of the project: Do the outcomes serve the purpose? Are we achieving what we set out to achieve?

4. Impact tells us whether or not we have bridged the gap in the problem we were seeking to address: Was the programme useful? Is it worth replicating?

5. Sustainability is measured by determining if the programme's benefits can be maintained over a long period of time.

Conclusion

The church today is living in an age of performance management systems, strategic management initiatives, and significant technological advances that highlight the potential influence of Christian work values. Qualities such as diligence, integrity, self-motivation, commitment, teamwork, and knowledge are greatly valued in the marketplace. A careful study of God's word reveals that such principles are central in forming a Christian worker. Therefore, there is a growing need for the church to strategically develop these values in a sustainable way so that we can account for the efforts of church workers and demonstrate the church's influence in the workplace. Whether youth are pursuing self-employment or seeking employment in established organizations, these values are vital for sustainable work performance.

In addition, the church must explore ideas and sound methodologies that have enabled corporates to grow in size, improve their work performances, and complete projects effectively and efficiently. Using such strategies in a church context can enable the church to be more efficient in what they do. Many churches have established professionally run projects to accomplish specific objectives, and a similar approach could be adopted to manage and monitor these projects. For example, what indicators would reveal if a worship team or a cell group is doing well? Does the church have documented expectations for these groups? Are these expectations communicated to both leaders and members of these groups?

It is my prayer that we would strive to work smarter in church and encourage our congregants to do the same.

Discussion Questions

1. Why should the church promote positive youth development and work?

2. How can the church equip youth for work in the community?

3. Describe the key elements of the church youth work model.

4. Why should focusing on God remain central in the church youth work model?

5. Why is sustainability crucial in the church youth work model?

6. What practical steps does the church and youth ministry need to take to implement the church youth work model?

Bibliography

Benson, P. L., and P. C. Scales. "Positive youth development and the prevention of youth aggression and violence." *International Journal of Developmental Science* 3, no. 3 (2009): 218–34.

Benson, Peter L., Peter C. Scales, Stephen F. Hamilton, and Arturo Sesma Jr. "Positive Youth Development: Theory, Research, and Applications." In *Handbook of Child psychology*, vol. 1, edited by William Damon and Richard Lerner. New York: Wiley & Sons, 2007.

Bloom, David E., Michael Kuhn, and Klaus Prettner. "Africa's Prospects for Enjoying a Demographic Dividend." *Journal of Demographic Economics* 83, no. 1 (2017): 63–76.

Brennan, Mark A., and Rosemary V. Barnett. "Bridging Community and Youth Development: Exploring Theory, Research, and Application." *Community Development* 40, no. 4 (2009): 305–10.

Butters, S., and S. Newell. *Realities of Training: a review of the training of adults who volunteer to work with young people in the Youth and Community Services.* Leicester: National Youth Bureau, 1978.

Campbell, David, and Nancy Erbstein. "Engaging Youth in Community Change: Three Key Implementation Principles." In *Innovative Community Change Practices*, edited by Norman Walzer and Sam Cordes, 72–88. Routledge, 2017.

Cooper, Trudi. "Models of Youth Work: A Framework for Positive Sceptical Reflection." *Youth and Policy* 109 (2012): 100–17.

Dev, Kapil. "Youth and Moral Values in a Changing Society." *International Journal of Advanced Research and Development* 2, no. 4 (2017): 164–67.

George, I. N., and U. D. Uyanga. "Youth and Moral Values in a Changing Society." *IOSR Journal of Humanities and Social Science* 19, no. 6 (2014): 40–44.

Glatzer, W., L. Camfield, V. Møller, and M. Rojas. *Global Handbook of Quality of Life. Exploration of Well-Being of Nations and Continents*. Dordrecht: Springer, 2015.

Kilonzo, Susan Mbula. "Youth, Religion, and Development in Africa." In *Religion and Development in Africa*, edited by Ezra Chitando, Masiiwa Ragies Gunda, and Lovemore Togarasei, 103–24. Bamberg: University of Bamberg Press, 2020.

Lerner, Jacqueline V., Erin Phelps, Yulika Forman, and Edmond P. Bowers. "Positive Youth Development." In *Individual Bases of Adolescent Development*, 524–58. Vol. 1 of *Handbook of Adolescent Psychology*, edited by Richard. M. Lerner and L. Steinberg. New York: Wiley & Sons, 2009.

Lerner, Richard M., Amy E. Alberts, Pamela M. Anderson, and Elizabeth M. Dowling. "On Making Humans Human: Spirituality and the Promotion of Positive Youth Development." In *The Handbook of Spiritual Development in Childhood and Adolescence*, edited by E. C. Roehlkepartain, P. E. King, L. Wagener, and P. L. Benson, 60–72. Thousand Oaks: SAGE, 2005.

Lerner, R. M., J. V. Lerner, S. Lewin-Bizan, E. P. Bowers, M. J. Boyd, M. K. Mueller, K. L. Schmid, and C. M. Napolitano. "Positive Youth Development: Processes, Programs, and Problematics." *Journal of Youth Development* 6, no. 3 (2011), 38–62.

Lerner, R. M., C. Brentano, E. M.Dowling, and P. M. Anderson. "Positive Youth Development: Thriving as the Basis of Personhood and Civil Society," *New Directions for Youth Development* 95 (2002), 11–34.

London, Jonathan K., Kristen Zimmerman, and Nancy Erbstein. "Youth-Led Research and Evaluation: Tools for Youth, Organizational, and Community Development." *New Directions for Evaluation* 98 (2003): 33–45.

Méndez, Elizabeth Tamez. "Positive Youth Development and Spirituality: From Theory to Research [review]." *Journal of Applied Christian Leadership* 4, no. 2 (2010): 74–78.

Møller, Valerie. "Quality of Life and Positive Youth Development in Grahamstown East, South Africa." In *Advances in Quality-of-Life Theory and Research*, edited by M. Joseph Sirgy, Don Rahtz, and A. Coskun Samli, 53–79. Dordrecht: Springer Netherlands, 2003.

Rocca, C., and I. Schultes. *Africa's Youth: Action Needed Now to Support the Continent's Greatest Asset*. Mo Ibrahim Foundation, 2020.

Smith, M. K. "From Youth Work to Youth Development: The New Government Framework for English Youth Services." *Youth and Policy* 79 (2003): 46–59.

5

Youth and Development: An Agenda for Church Praxis and Human Flourishing

Barnabé Anzuruni Msabah

Abstract

Development is a multidimensional concept, often difficult to define precisely, and the notion of "youth" is equally broad and subject to ongoing debate. In the African context, the complexity is even more. The reality of today's African youth is marked by stark contrasts and profound inequalities – economic, technological, social, and cultural – that vary considerably depending on factors such as family background, country of origin, and even region within a given country. At the same time, Africa is undergoing a radical demographic transformation, with the youngest and most dynamic population in the world. This "youth bulge" highlights not only the urgency of addressing the rights and aspirations of young people, but also the immense potential they represent as agents of transformation. If their needs continue to be ignored or unmet, this demographic asset could quickly turn into a socioeconomic burden – a missed opportunity with serious consequences. In light of this, we must ask urgent and critical questions about the place and role of this growing youth demographic in Africa's development agenda. Are young people being empowered as full participants in shaping the future of the continent? What structures and mindsets need to change – in the church, in policy, and in society at large – to ensure they are not only included but equipped and trusted to lead? This chapter attempts to answer these and many other questions by exploring the complex realities facing African youth today and examining how the church, in partnership with wider society, can empower young people to be active contributors to holistic and sustainable development across the continent.

Introduction

There is no universally accepted definition of youth. Some propose that the term "youth" is a sociocultural construct defined by a series of indicators such as age, marital status, and financial independence or dependence.[1] However, these indicators vary considerably across cultures and contexts. Although the United Nations defines youth as people between the ages of eighteen and twenty-four, many researchers argue for an age range of eighteen to forty, or even forty-five. This vague definition of youth in terms of chronological age is a matter of dispute among scholars.[2] Thus, most researchers agree that the concept of youth is better defined based on their capacity to act rather than age group.[3] The term "youth" – like "development" – is a complex term that remains difficult to define.

Against this background, one of the sad realities in Africa is that young people make up 60 percent of the continent's unemployed population.[4] This is why youth must remain at the heart of the church's efforts to bring about transformational change in communities. This chapter seeks to emphasize this critical aspect, while acknowledging the pervasive impact of poverty across the continent.

It is also important to bear in mind the diversity among African youth and their varying motivations. Africa is culturally, socially, economically, politically, ecologically, and spiritually diverse.[5] Therefore, human development – including that of youth – must consider the diverse values, aspirations, and social contexts that shape individual choices. This means there are multiple motivations for young people's development choices, which should be understood within their specific contexts.[6] It further means that a one-size-fits-all approach to development is inadequate, and that meaningful development must consider the diverse motivations and contexts of individuals, including youth.

---

1. Ho, Clarke, and Dougherty, "Youth-Led Social Change," 54; Afifi, "Youth as Agents of Change," 11.

2. Fien, Neil, and Bentley, "Youth Can Lead," 57; Kasumagic, "Engaging Youth," 384.

3. Balcomb, "What Theology?," 6.

4. Tolman et al., "Youth Acts," 79.

5. Flanagan and Sherrod, "Youth Political Development," 449.

6. Deneulin and Davies, "Theology and Development," 4.

The purpose of this chapter is to show that, from a transformational development viewpoint, the country's future depends on its youth. Young people should no longer be viewed merely as beneficiaries of development aid but, rather, as key assets for sustainable development. The chapter also demonstrates that young people are not merely the leaders of tomorrow – as often claimed – but also the leaders of today. Addressing the problems of African societies requires a critical and pragmatic African theology that is grounded in concrete and effective Christian commitment. Such an approach will enable the process of transformational development to become a sustainable reality that is driven by the continent's youth.

Youth as Major Players in the Development Agenda

Talking about youth from a transformational development perspective is a complex and diverse task because the current situation of African youth is characterized by significant paradoxes and stark disparities. On one hand, Africa has the world's youngest population and enormous human potential. On the other, youth face high unemployment, exclusion from policy-making, and often live in fragile social and economic systems. This reality demands not just programmes for youth, but programmes with youth at the centre as agents of transformation. As Fulford and Thompson observe, "Although many youth programs see marginalized adolescents as a problem, youth become the problem solvers in youth community development programs."[7] This shift from viewing youth as passive recipients to recognizing them as co-creators of community well-being directly addresses the paradox of marginalization despite potential. It invites African practitioners and policymakers to adopt models that dismantle disempowering narratives and instead promote youth-led, context-relevant change, especially in sectors like agriculture, ecology, and social cohesion. The demographic weight of this young population highlights the crucial role of youth in Africa's development process. However, this demographic growth could turn into a nightmare if urgent action is not taken to meet the needs and aspirations of this growing population. Young people in Africa have the talent and creativity to find new solutions to African problems. However, to realize their full potential, they require support and equal opportunities.

The film *The Boy Who Harnessed the Wind* is the true story of fourteen-year-old William Kamkwamba from rural Malawi. Although forced to quit

---

7. Fulford and Thompson, "Youth Community Gardening," 57.

school because of a drought that caused his family's crops to fail and his entire community to suffer from hunger, William managed to get access to the school library. Despite his poor knowledge of English, and with only the help of a translating dictionary, he read books on electrical engineering and energy production and taught himself the basic principles of power generation. Driven by a desire to help those affected by the drought in his village, this young boy used parts from bicycles and other scrap materials to design and build a full-size wind turbine, powerful enough to run lights and water pumps for his poor village in Malawi. Although his family, friends, and other members of the community initially doubted him, eventually, they helped William to build this windmill. This young boy's invention brought light to the homes of the villagers, enabled them to recharge their phones and radios, and powered their water pumps so that they could water their crops, thus saving the village from famine.

The story of William Kamkwamba is just one of many examples that show how youth can be active participants in transformational development. Young people are often overlooked, misunderstood, or even ignored, but their energy, ideas, and resourcefulness are vital to us all in our rapidly changing world. According to the *World Youth Report*, as of 2019, the world was home to 1.8 billion young people aged fifteen to twenty-four, which represents about 16 percent of the global population.[8] These youth are generally full of energy and ideas, and many are developing their skills, enjoying life, and contributing to society. Therefore, it is essential to critically examine the place and role of this growing youth population in the development of the African continent from a theological perspective.

The problems faced by African societies demand that practical theology be both critical and pragmatic, and must be rooted in an authentic, active Christian witness that transforms lives because the mission and nature of the church have their source in the mission and nature of God.[9] This will allow our transformational development process to be a sustainable reality, which is why discussions about development in the twenty-first century cannot ignore the contribution of youth. With over two hundred million people aged fifteen to twenty-four, Africa has the largest youth population in the world.[10] Many African youth, in search of better opportunities, risk their lives by attempting to cross the Mediterranean Sea to reach Europe – often in overcrowded and

---

8. United Nations, *World Youth Report*.
9. Balcomb, "What Theology?," 6; Anderson, *Shape of Practical Theology*, 31.
10. United Nations, *World Youth Report*.

unsafe boats. Thousands perish in the process due to drowning, exploitation, or harsh conditions. Although young Africans are pushed by socio-economic and political conditions to leave their homelands out of desperation, they were not born to die chasing opportunities abroad in such dangerous ways. Studies suggest that Africa's youth population is likely to double in the next twenty-five years, which means that the church has an opportunity to engage in inclusive economic transformation programmes that target youth on the continent.[11] This population growth is a development opportunity for the continent, particularly in the areas of innovation and social transformation, since 60 percent of Africa's population is under the age of twenty-four.[12]

By 2050, it is projected that 35 percent of the world's youth will be African, which is why young people are mobilizing their peers to speak out on issues that affect their dignity and future.[13] This trend is important for the future of this continent, and this youthful population can be harnessed to boost economic productivity and bring about equitable social and industrial transformation. According to the World Bank, such actions could help Africa eradicate poverty, protect the planet, and foster well-being and prosperity, which is why evidence of youth-focused community change is increasingly visible in the lives of empowered young people, more responsive institutions, inclusive local policies, and tangible improvements in community well-being.[14] Since youth represent Africa's greatest opportunity to combine creativity and innovation, we must find ways to support young Africans as they engage in income-generating activities that will not only enable them to meet their daily needs but also improve their livelihoods and well-being. With many youth seeking greener pastures outside Africa, the country faces the serious problem of brain drain. To address this issue, it is crucial to ensure that all young people, regardless of background or gender, are given opportunities to succeed. This is another reason the church should prioritize youth engagement.

Africa's future depends on how well we harness and support the energy and involvement of young people. Yet, demographic shifts alone cannot drive the continent's progress. Sustainable development hinges on proactive policies

---

11. See, for example, United Nations, *World Youth Report*; International Labour Organization, *Global Employment Trends*.

12. United Nations, *World Youth Report*; International Labour Organization, *Global Employment Trends*.

13. United Nations, *World Youth Report*; International Labour Organization, *Global Employment Trends*; Beukes and Van der Westhuizen, "Demarginalising Youths," 5.

14. World Bank, *End Extreme Poverty*; see also Campbell and Erbstein, "Engaging Youth," 70; Makhoul, Alameddine, and Afifi, "I Felt," 921.

and a combination of factors – such as higher enrollment rates paired with quality education, a resilient healthcare system, and economic conditions that foster growth and job creation.[15] As Garcia and Jean highlight, revitalizing the labour market and enhancing youth employability is critical.[16] This requires aligning education and training with labour market demands, particularly in emerging sectors.[17] Innovation would enable Africa to navigate its development stages while creating the required jobs for its youth population.

Innovation is essential for Africa's sustainable development, particularly in addressing the urgent need for job creation among its rapidly growing youth population.[18] Traditional development strategies alone cannot meet the demands of this demographic shift. Innovation enables young people to become job creators rather than job seekers, empowering them to contribute meaningfully to their communities. However, achieving this potential depends on implementing sound policies and investing in human capital sectors such as higher education, vocational training, skills development, agriculture and food security, health, job creation, promotion of entrepreneurship, and peace and security.[19] In other words, effective policies and measures are essential to take advantage of demographic benefits. The church cannot work in isolation when it comes to involving youth in Africa's development. Community transformation is a shared responsibility that thrives through active collaboration among the church, civil society, government, private sector, and other partners. These stakeholders can create meaningful opportunities for young people to participate in and shape the future of their communities.[20] Young people must be involved in identifying their own priorities and partnering with development actors to ensure the successful implementation of the various development initiatives.

If young Africans are skilled and employable, and if African economies embrace competition, the continent could become an important centre for

---

15. Filmer and Fox, *Youth Employment*, 76.

16. Garcia and Fares, *Youth in Africa's Labor Market*, 44.

17. Garcia and Fares, 46.

18. Demi, McLaughlin, and Snyder, "Rural Youth," 311; Delgado and Staples, *Youth-Led Community Organizing*, 47.

19. Delgado, *Social Youth Entrepreneurship*, 61.

20. Ho, Clarke, and Dougherty, "Youth-Led Social Change"; Kasumagic, "Engaging Youth," 375–92.

job creation in the near future.[21] However, if today's youth remain unqualified, unskilled, and inexperienced, Africa will be dysfunctional and its economy will remain trapped in exploitative capitalism, leading to increased misery and hopelessness among its people. By involving young people in the development agenda, we engage people with fresh ideas, an eagerness to work, and a keen desire to stand up for what is right. By giving them a platform and a voice, we are investing in the present and preparing our countries for a brighter future.

In promoting youth participation in development, the church has a vital role to play in facilitating spaces where young people are empowered as agents of transformation in their communities. This aligns with Fulford and Thompson's observation that youth empowerment initiatives can serve as models for community revitalization, noting that "youth-serving agencies, community development organizations, and government policy makers could look to the YEA [Youth Engagement and Action] as a model for youth empowerment and community revitalization."[22] In the African context – where youth make up the majority population and often face exclusion from decision-making structures – the church can replicate similar models by engaging youth in community-based agricultural, ecological, or sanitation projects. These initiatives can serve not only as platforms for leadership development and social engagement but also as vehicles for healing and holistic transformation, grounded in the church's mission of justice and renewal. The Youth Engagement and Action (YEA) model empowers young people for community development through participation and leadership. It enables them to be co-creators and leaders in transformative initiatives, partnering with community and faith organizations to drive social change. The YEA model focuses on empowering youth to address community issues, fostering collaboration with adults and organizations, and facilitating a youth-led transformational development.

African Youth and the Development Challenge

Many young Africans face an uncertain future. Each month, ten million youth reach working age, but there are not enough jobs for all of them.[23] A recent report on youth employment by the International Labour Organization indi-

---

21. Brennan, "Conceptualizing Resiliency," 59; Garcia and Fares, *Youth in Africa's Labor Market*, 28; Brennan, Barnett, and Baugh, "Youth Involvement," 210; Balsano, "Youth Civic Engagement," 191; Bogenschneider, "Ecological Risk," 134.

22. Fulford and Thompson, "Youth Community Gardening," 56.

23. United Nations, *World Youth Report*.

cates that young people are twice as likely to be unemployed as adults.[24] Other pressures faced by youth include lack of education, poverty, early marriage, conflict, corruption, political uncertainty, and environmental degradation. When discussing transformational development in Africa, it is also important to consider the realities of a growing population, an overloaded education system, and the unemployment of this available and active youth population.[25] If prompt action is not taken to meet the needs and aspirations of this growing population, the demographic opportunity could shift from being the driver of transformation to becoming a major social and economic crisis.

Demographic trends in Africa show that the population is growing faster than in any other region of the world.[26] This unique demographic profile will have far-reaching consequences for the continent and highlights the importance of job creation for Africa's youth.

Since Africa's youth population is growing rapidly, it is important to identify the factors that influence the development decisions of this fast-growing population and the challenges that limit their ability to contribute meaningfully to the development process.[27] These young people are not merely starting businesses out of necessity or survival instinct. Rather, their engagement in entrepreneurial ventures and community development is often deeply inspired and nurtured by the presence of positive role models. When youth observe individuals they admire – whether successful entrepreneurs, community leaders, or mentors – demonstrating commitment to societal transformation, they are more likely to envision their own capacity to make a meaningful impact. Role models provide more than motivation; they embody what is possible, offering guidance, encouragement, and a framework for ethical leadership and sustainable innovation. In this sense, fostering visible, accessible, and values-driven role models within African communities and churches becomes a critical strategy in mobilizing youth to actively contribute to the development agenda with purpose and confidence. However, the sustained presence of poverty and the deepening gap between the rich and the poor continue to obstruct meaningful progress across the continent.[28] Therefore, a new development framework is needed to address the structural causes and systemic drivers of

---

24. International Labour Organization, *Global Employment Trends*, 126–27.

25. Filmer and Fox, *Youth Employment*, 29.

26. Delgado and Staples, *Youth-Led Community Organizing*, 17; Balsano, "Youth Civic Engagement," 190; Tolman et al., "Youth Acts," 22.

27. Brennan, Barnett, and McGrath, "Intersection of Youth," 334.

28. Camino, "Youth-Led Community Building," 5.

poverty, inequality, and social injustices and, thereby, to create conditions for a viable future from a transformational development perspective.

Africa's demographic asset also constitutes an economic and social challenge that has implications for peace and security.[29] The youth unemployment rate in Africa is the highest in the world.[30] In addition to the combination of high unemployment, underemployment, and poverty, there are also the problems of insufficient access to education, health services, and other facilities, as well as extreme vulnerability to conflict and violence.[31] This combination of factors has destabilized several African countries and enlarged the ranks of disillusioned and neglected young people, who could well become potential recruits for extremist groups. While Africa's demographic structure presents great opportunities, it also carries risks such as unemployment, underemployment, and the lack of social security, educational opportunities, and inclusive governance.[32] This in turn may lead to young people engaging in activities that increase their vulnerability – for instance, involvement in terrorist organizations or illegal migration. A large population of unemployed youth can, therefore, lead to political instability or even conflict.

Large urban centres, which are undoubtedly popular destinations for many young people seeking opportunities, are facing increasing difficulties in managing mega-slums that continue to grow in most African countries.[33] Unless political leaders create adequate opportunities for young people to earn a decent living, the resulting frustrations – like widespread unemployment – may push them toward dangerous alternatives that exploit their vulnerability and offer them a false sense of purpose.[34] These are dangerous causes or ideologies that exploit the frustration of unemployed or marginalized youth, offering them a false sense of purpose, belonging, or reward but which appeal to young people who feel abandoned or hopeless. The growing African youth population could become a demographic time bomb.[35]

---

29. Ginwright and James, "Assets to Agents," 27–46.

30. Filmer and Fox, *Youth Employment*, 28.

31. Bradley, Deighton, and Selby, "'Voices' Project," 208.

32. Heath, *ArtShow*, 115.

33. Brennan and Barnett, "Bridging Community," 307.

34. Filmer and Fox, *Youth Employment*, 49; Flanagan and Sherrod, "Youth Political Development," 450.

35. Christens and Dolan, "Interweaving Youth Development," 534; Allen et al., "Suicide Prevention," 282.

As inequalities and disparities continue to increase, transformational development in Africa requires mobilizing various resources.[36] Income inequality in Africa is higher than in any other region of the world. Even if the number of people living in absolute poverty decreases over time, inequalities and disparities will remain a major concern for Africa. There have been considerable improvements in access to basic services such as education, health, and sanitation.[37] However, this overall improvement often masks disparities related to gender, rural or urban status, and family income levels.[38] In development practice, not all inequality is unjust. Some distinctions, such as those based on differences in skills, education, or effort, may be acceptable or even necessary for functioning societies. However, development practitioners and scholars widely agree that the high and growing levels of inequality found in much of Africa are unjustified. These disparities often reflect structural injustices, historical disadvantages, and policy failures, making them deeply unfair and harmful to sustainable and inclusive development. Extreme income disparities slow the pace of poverty reduction and hinder the process of development. An increase in inequality is likely to cause social unrest, ranging from possible collapse in fragile countries such as the Great Lakes region to increased social tension in more stable countries, leading to large population movements across borders.[39] Since development has a significant impact on poverty, and given the dimensions of the problem, increasing opportunities for the most vulnerable is the only way to both support transformation and reduce disparities. While employment can serve as a means for youth to escape poverty, it is also vital to address the disparities in access to quality education, health, and other services. Many young people, especially those from marginalized or disadvantaged communities, do not have the same level of access to essential services that can help them thrive. For example, some youth may attend under-resourced schools with poorly trained teachers or lack access to digital tools and learning materials, while others benefit from high-quality education. In terms of health, disparities may include limited access to clinics, clean water, or reproductive health services, leading to preventable illnesses or early school dropout – especially for girls. These inequalities are often influenced

---

36. United Nations, *Recovering Better*; Conner and Cosner, "Youth Change Agents," 2.

37. Checkoway, "What Is Youth Participation?," 342.

38. Brennan, Barnett, and Lesmeister, "Enhancing Local Capacity," 20; Checkoway and Gutierrez, "Youth Participation," 6.

39. Campbell and Erbstein, "Engaging Youth," 71; James and McGillicuddy, "Building Youth Movements," 2.

by factors such as geographic location, economic status, gender, or disability, and they limit the potential of young people to fully participate in and benefit from development processes.

In addressing the widespread issue of youth unemployment in Africa, churches and development actors can play a pivotal role by equipping young people with relevant life skills, agro-entrepreneurship training, and green skills. Such initiatives align with approaches that emphasize the development of general competencies and behaviours necessary for securing meaningful employment and achieving long-term personal and professional goals as observed by Fulford and Thompson.[40] Linking skills training to local, income-generating projects not only builds capacity but also restores dignity and instills hope among youth.

The Church's Role in Promoting Youth Participation in the Development Agenda

Every year, thousands of desperate young people lose their lives in the Mediterranean while attempting to escape poverty and its fatal consequences on the African continent. The current trend of out-migration to the West among African youth is evidence of this reality, revealing that Africa is pushing away its hope and exporting its resources without receiving anything in return. That is to say, Africa invests in its youth, but when they migrate, the benefits of that investment are enjoyed elsewhere. There is little to no return on investment for Africa when the educated and skilled youth migrate to the West and settle there permanently. The continent often invests heavily in education, healthcare, and development of its young population, but loses the potential economic, social, and leadership contributions they could have made locally. There can be some indirect return on investment, for example, through remittances, knowledge transfer, or diaspora engagement in development initiatives. But these benefits often do not match the value of what is lost when talented youth leave permanently, especially if they become disconnected from their home countries.

Since the future of the continent is at stake, the church in Africa must be intentional about reversing this trend by being involved in efforts to prevent forced migration of the continent's most precious asset. If youth in Africa are meaningfully engaged within the sustainable development sector, African countries could occupy prominent places in the ranking of economically established countries. In other words, Africa has great potential, given its youthful

---

40. Fulford and Thompson, "Youth Community Gardening," 66.

population and its natural resources, which are vital and sustainable assets for transformational development. The church must rise as a transformative agent that empowers young people to flourish within the continent. The church can create viable alternatives to migration by investing in youth economic empowerment through skills training, entrepreneurship support, and mentorship. The church should also advocate for education systems that align with market realities while forming godly character and purpose. In addition, the church must use its prophetic voice to challenge corruption and injustice – key push factors driving migration – while nurturing platforms for youth leadership, civic engagement, and holistic discipleship that speaks to body, mind, and spirit.

Besides, the church can mobilize the African Christian diaspora to reinvest their skills and resources back home through mentoring, knowledge exchange, and development partnerships. It is time the church helps the youth reimagine their future as builders of their communities rather than seekers of escape by cultivating a theology of hope in abundant Africa, a theology of rootedness in purpose, etc. In this way, the church does not only respond to brain drain but reshapes the narrative – revealing that Africa's greatest resource is not being lost, but being released into redemptive action.

Delgado and Staples argue that effective public policies are vital to improve working conditions in Africa.[41] The youth have a key role to play in breathing new life into civil society, particularly through organized groups or networks formed around shared interests, goals, or identities – such as youth groups, community-based organizations, student unions, faith-based networks, cooperatives, or issue-driven movements. These associations are crucial components of civil society because they provide platforms for civic engagement, collective action, advocacy, community service, and social innovation. Culture and sport, which are areas of interest for many young people, are also important avenues for personal development and social cohesion, especially in regions plagued by violence or armed conflict, such as the Great Lakes region of Africa. To address the development challenges faced by youth, the church must identify activities that interest youth – for example, sports. Participation in sports can greatly improve young people's physical and emotional health. It can also increase confidence, promote positive involvement in society, and foster a sense of hope for the future. Through sports, youth learn key values such as honesty, teamwork, fair play, respect for others, and the importance of following rules. They also learn how to deal with competition and cope with both winning and losing.

---

41. Delgado and Staples, *Youth-Led Community Organizing*, 23; see also Flanagan and Sherrod, "Youth Political Development," 450.

Sport is an appealing activity for young people and can serve as a good foundation for peacebuilding, health, and education. One of the most obvious benefits of sports is good physical health. Exercise can lower the risks of obesity, heart disease, diabetes, and other medical conditions. Through sports programmes, the church can educate youth about healthy eating habits, sexual health, and the dangers of smoking, drugs, and alcohol. Physical activity can reduce anxiety levels and enhance feelings of well-being and self-esteem. In addition, being able to talk through problems with friends and older role models from the church can help young people find their own solutions to troubling issues. For young people who have experienced trauma – caused by bereavement, war, violence, rejection, or a natural disaster – sports can play an important role in their recovery. Exercise, friendships, fun, and the chance to talk about their concerns with someone can help youth to come to terms with difficult experiences. Sports is a social activity and a good way for young people to connect with one another in a safe environment. Friendship and having a common focus fosters a sense of belonging. Team sports such as football teach young people how to manage conflict and control their emotions even when things are not going their way. Finally, fair play and the ability to follow rules are important life skills that youth can learn through sports.

Practical theology of development is more than merely providing a well, a school, or a hospital. Rather, it is about building communities, tackling the root causes of poverty, and building resilience. It is about encouraging parents to send their children – both boys and girls – to school. It is about creating employment opportunities for both youth and adults.[42] It is about finding out what a community needs and how best to meet those needs.[43] And it is about creating space for young people to be proactively involved in this whole process. The church can play a key role in enabling communities to live with justice, dignity, peace, and hope.

From a practical theology of development perspective, youth is not understood merely as an age category, but rather as a distinct standing – a spiritual positioning and predisposition before God. This is because youth represents a unique relational posture marked by energy, openness, identity formation, and a longing for justice and purpose. Youth is therefore a season where individuals are more receptive to God's call and capable of bold, imaginative faith. This "standing" includes both a predisposition – such as curiosity, vulnerability, and spiritual responsiveness – and a positioning, as seen throughout Scripture,

42. Filmer and Fox, *Youth Employment*, 21.
43. Beukes and Van der Westhuizen, "Demarginalising Youths," 4.

where God entrusts young people like Joseph (Gen 37:5–11; 41:46), David (1 Sam 16:12–13; 17:33–37), Jeremiah (Jer 1:4–10), and Mary (Luke 1:26–38) with significant roles in his redemptive purposes. These examples reflect the theological reality that God often entrusts young people with significant responsibilities, showing that age is not a barrier to fulfilling God's purpose.

Youth, then, is not defined by immaturity but by potential; it is a sacred life stage through which God often initiates renewal, transformation, and hope. The church must therefore recognize, nurture, and release this standing – not merely ministering to youth, but walking with them as co-agents of God's mission in the world.[44] Youth is inseparable or inherently linked to our human condition and is an integral part of our identity before God. It is that special kairos moment, the opportune moment for love and acceptance, dreams and hopes, the search for meaning, enthusiasm, activity, creativity, and hopefulness.[45] It is because of this understanding that practical theology reflects on the mutual relationship between the temporality of youth and the eternality of God in order to determine how young people can participate in the process of transformational development. To be young is, therefore, to anticipate the future with hope.[46] While hope is a gift to all humanity, it is especially vibrant in youth, who often carry a deep desire for change, justice, and a better future. Their hope is not just optimism – it is a spiritual resource that reflects God's work in them and through them. The church has a significant role in recognizing and nurturing this hope, creating space for young people to lead, serve, and contribute meaningfully to God's mission. As Joel 2:28 reminds us, youth are bearers of vision—a sign that the Holy Spirit is moving. The church is a place where hope is not only preached, but lived out through the passion and action of its younger members.

Since youth represent a significant portion of the African population, it is essential to involve them in development decisions and the implementation of development programmes. Doing so will strengthen their role in promoting social change. African youth need to actively participate in all decisions affecting their present and future, and the church should support youth in their efforts to abolish the sociopolitical and economic barriers that make them passive actors in development. The church has a responsibility to partner with the youth of Africa and take the lead in guiding the continent towards the glory and greatness of the socio-economic independence of its young people

---

44. Beukes and Van der Westhuizen, 6.
45. Checkoway, "What Is Youth Participation?," 342.
46. Bauman, "To Hope Is Human," 65.

and the transformational development of communities. Only then can Africa achieve its aspirations and fulfil its development agenda.

The church in Africa has a critical role in creating spaces where youth are not only heard but actively involved in shaping their communities. By facilitating youth participation in development processes, the church helps to disrupt unequal power dynamics and foster a sense of shared responsibility and leadership. In contexts where young people represent the majority of the population, especially in Africa, their engagement is not optional – it is essential. Through intentional discipleship, mentorship, and community-based initiatives, the church can empower youth to become co-labourers in God's mission of transformation and justice. The ability of youth participation to shift power dynamics is not unique to Africa; as Fulford and Thompson note in the Canadian context, youth-led development programs also create space for young people to influence power structures and actively contribute to community transformation.[47] The importance of young people in development cannot be overemphasized.[48] Yet many local church leaders in Africa fail to understand the needs of young people and are unable to effectively engage them. Youth is a time of unprecedented challenges, which may be why Paul urges Timothy to "flee the evil desires of youth" (2 Tim 2:22). God treasures the passion, boldness, and forward-looking vision of young people, and they have an invaluable part to play in the service of God and the nation. In his old age, Solomon – who wasted much of his youth – urges people to remember their Creator in their youth (Eccl 12:1). Similarly, Paul urges Timothy, his friend and mentee, never to allow anyone to despise him on account of his youth but, instead, to be an example in all matters of faith and conduct (1 Tim 4:12). Paul understood the role and value of young people and affirmed that, when properly mentored, they can be positive role models. The Bible gives many examples of how God entrusted youth with the tasks of social transformation and nation-building and appointed them to vital roles in carrying out his wonderful plan of redemption. This same God will also use the young people of today to fulfil his glorious plan on the African continent. The youth in Africa have great potential and are an important human resource that God can use.

The African Youth Charter aims to empower young people to drive development across the continent.[49] The church should join forces with civil society to ensure that the Charter is implemented and that it is supported and ratified

---

47. Fullford and Thompson, "Youth Community Gardening," 57.
48. Youniss and Reinders, "Youth and Community Service," 242.
49. Afifi, "Youth as Agents of Change," 11.

by local authorities. There is, therefore, much work for the church to do in areas such as job creation, sustainable livelihoods, education, health, and youth participation. However, it is essential that young people also develop entrepreneurial skills that will aid the church in promoting science, technology, engineering, mathematics, and entrepreneurship within its various congregations.

Young people must take an active role in all the decisions that affect their present and future. Their intellectual contributions and capacity for mobilization provide unique perspectives on how to strengthen their role as active participants in promoting the economic and social development agenda.[50] This is why the local church, in consultation with youth, should establish a framework that promotes dialogue between young people and various stakeholders, creating mechanisms for youth to express their views on decisions taken about them. In addition, local churches should ensure that over half of their young people – both boys and girls – are enrolled in schools and receive appropriate education or equivalent professional training. This must go hand in hand with mechanisms that involve young people in all the decision-making processes of the church so that they can gain experience and be challenged to improve. To ensure that youth are viewed as assets for transformational development, local churches must fight human rights violations against youth and equip them with the necessary skills and resources,[51] thereby enabling them to realize their full potential and achieve their economic and social aspirations.

In light of this, it is imperative that the church support and train young people because they are vital to transformational development. Many young people in Africa feel excluded, and this often leads to the loss of their own values and identity.[52] To avoid this feeling of being socially excluded, youth often compromise their cultural identity in an attempt to integrate into the dominant culture because their identity is shaped by interactions with others and a sense of belonging to various groups, associations, and movements, both inside and outside the church.[53] The church can serve as a healing space that demonstrates that there is enough room for everyone to nurture their talents and develop their visions. Young people need ideal, consistent, and authentic mentors if they are to become assets for social transformation and integral

---

50. Garcia and Fares, *Youth in Africa's Labor Market*, 61; Hung, "East New York Farms," 66; Bradley, Deighton, and Selby, "'Voices' Project," 203.

51. Ginwright and James, "Assets to Agents," 33.

52. Checkoway, "What Is Youth Participation?," 342.

53. Autry and Anderson, "Recreation," 269; James and McGillicuddy, "Building Youth Movements," 2.

development.[54] Young people need mentors who embody the wisdom of African communal values and the integrity of Christian discipleship – elders and leaders who walk with them consistently, model authentic living, and guide them toward becoming agents of social transformation and holistic development.

The role of youth in advancing the kingdom of God and transforming communities must be highlighted within both the church and society. Young people are not only part of today's church membership but should also be part of its leadership. To confine young people to the label of "leaders of tomorrow" is to diminish their current value and agency; it is to silence their contributions in the present, and this risks marginalising them in the efforts to shape Africa's development today.

Therefore, the church must build bridges between the present and the future by creating accessible and inclusive spaces for youth.[55] It is the responsibility of local churches to initiate discussions about the future of youth in Africa. Such discussions and urgent actions are essential for creating livelihoods for young people. For example, the church could establish a youth development fund to support young people's entrepreneurial initiatives. Ecclesial youth development funds can support the employment of young people across different development sectors. Supporting young people through internships, professional programmes, and training is essential, and such initiatives can be spearheaded by the church. Since youth have so much potential, they should never be underestimated or ignored. Partnering with the youth is fundamental for sustainable, integral, and transformational development.

It is important to recognize that the youth of this continent can become what they aspire to be within the limits of God's will. They only need to be encouraged to find their identity in Christ and mentored to align their vision with God's will and purpose. Young people need to know who they are in Christ and what they represent, and by helping them to understand their identity and purpose in life, the church will have taken a major step in mentoring and empowering them. The church should inspire youth to take on leadership positions that contribute to the development of various sectors in the African continent. Today, Pan-Africanism involves engaging African youth in discussions about sustainable and integral development. A promising future is possible if we unite around the ideal that my development is also your development. The church should encourage young people to challenge socio-economic injustices

---

54. Beukes and Van der Westhuizen, "Demarginalising Youths," 7.

55. Beukes and Van der Westhuizen; Becker, Randels, and Theodore, "Project BRAVE," 46.

through entrepreneurship, community action, or some other development activity. The church should also recognize the potential of youth and work with them to raise awareness and set transformational development goals for their own community. However, the church cannot achieve a great deal on its own; therefore, it is essential that both the private and public sectors also commit to supporting such initiatives through partnerships with local churches to build a better future for the next generation.[56]

Engaging with young people – both inside and outside the church – is not an easy task. Therefore, the church should provide young people with opportunities to take on meaningful roles in the development and implementation of youth programmes, thereby ensuring their full participation. In other words, young people should take ownership of development opportunities that facilitate their own success. To develop a strategic plan that includes young people as part of the transformational development process within communities, the church will need to promote dialogue with them and jointly assess development plans and programmes.[57] The church has a responsibility to support or even directly provide alternative educational opportunities – especially in contexts where formal state education is inaccessible, inadequate, or unjust. Alternative opportunities could be church-run schools, vocational training, literacy programs, discipleship schools, or informal learning spaces that equip young people holistically. This will only be possible if the church ensures that education addresses the socio-economic needs of young people and continuously emphasizes concepts such as environmental protection, sustainable development, and new methods for strengthening skills practices throughout their schooling.[58] In addition, the church should support youth programmes, projects, and networks and encourage young people to participate not just in projects of their choice but also in the conception, design, application, monitoring, and evaluation of projects.

Engaging youth in community-based initiatives such as urban gardens or environmental restoration projects can transform not only their perception of themselves but also the way their communities regard them. Evidence suggests that such involvement fosters pride, a sense of accomplishment, and more positive attitudes toward local communities.[59] In many African urban contexts where young people often face neglect or negative stereotyping, giving

---

56. Barnett and Brennan, "Integrating Youth," 11.
57. Boyd et al., "Harnessing the Social Capital," 191.
58. Ansell, *Children, Youth and Development*, 209.
59. Fulford and Thompson, 69.

them stewardship over shared public spaces can serve as a powerful tool for social transformation.

Conclusion

Africa's burgeoning youth population represents a defining force for the continent's future; one that offers immense opportunities for transformation, yet also poses significant challenges. For the church and youth ministries, this demographic shift is both a call and a gift: a call to reimagine youth ministry as a space of empowerment and leadership development, and a gift of energy, creativity, and resilience. Rather than viewing young people as passive recipients of development interventions, they must be recognized as active agents whose participation is vital to the sustainability and effectiveness of Africa's development agenda. However, structural barriers – ranging from unemployment, political exclusion, inadequate education systems, and economic inequality – continue to limit youth engagement across the continent. The church is uniquely positioned to respond to these limitations through theologically grounded, contextually relevant initiatives that promote justice, dignity, diversity and inclusion. By nurturing spaces where young people can lead, innovate, and participate meaningfully, the church not only fulfills its pastoral mandate but also contributes to holistic transformation. Empowering youth to own and shape development processes ensures not only more sustainable outcomes but also a deeper alignment with the values of the Kingdom of God – where everyone, especially the young, are seen, heard, and sent.

In God's eyes, youth is not just a stage of life – it is a vital part of how we grow, serve, and relate to him. God called and empowered young people – like David, Jeremiah, and Mary – not despite their age, but because of their readiness to respond in faith. As the church we have a responsibility to do more than minister to young people – we must walk with them, make room for their leadership, and trust that God is speaking and working through them. This is because the youth are not the church of tomorrow; they are an important and meaningful part of the Body of Christ today, called to help shape God's mission of transformation in our communities. In the same way, within the context of theology and development practice, youth are not just beneficiaries of projects – they are essential partners in transformation. Ignoring their contributions weakens both social progress and spiritual depth.

Development that is transformative and holistic must have space for youth to participate, lead, and shape solutions. Faith-based organizations and NGOs have a unique opportunity to empower youth not only with skills, but with platforms for action, voice, and co-ownership of the development agenda. Youth must be understood as a theological category – marked by openness, prophetic vision, and moral agency. They represent a unique standing before God, often positioned in Scripture (e.g. 1 Sam 17; Jer 1:6–8; Luke 1:26–38) as catalysts for divine action and social renewal. We are therefore invited to affirm youth as subjects of transformation, not just objects of formation. To engage youth theologically is to affirm their role as co-labourers in God's vineyard, holding together vocation, justice, and spiritual identity in the life of the church and the world.

Young people have a great deal to contribute to society. It is essential that we listen to them and provide the support they need to shape both the present and the future. Our youth are not just the future; they are the present. When we provide them with the right tools, they will make a difference, and we will see our communities and countries flourish. The church needs to mentor young people in order to provide them with the skills they need to address social, economic, and environmental concerns in our communities. Digital technology, especially the internet, has transformed the world we live in. Across the globe, young people are the most connected segment of the population. According to the *World Youth Report*, nearly three-quarters of young people use the internet, compared to about half of the overall population.[60] The internet offers opportunities for young people to learn, socialize, find employment, and make their voices heard. As people interact online, barriers associated with age, gender, ethnicity, disability, wealth, and status are broken down. It could be said that the harvest is online, but the workers are offline.

In today's digital age, the opportunities for ministry, advocacy, education, and community transformation have increasingly moved online. Social media platforms, digital storytelling, virtual learning environments, and mobile technology offer immense potential for spreading the gospel, engaging youth, and influencing development agendas. Yet, many churches and Christian youth across Africa remain significantly underrepresented in these digital spaces, which is a missed opportunity. While social media platforms shape opinions and drive social movements, many African Christians are either absent or passive consumers rather than active creators and influencers. The digital field is ripe with people seeking truth, hope, identity, and community – yet the church's presence is often minimal or reactive.

Equipping African youth for digital evangelism and discipleship is crucial. Churches should offer digital literacy training, potentially partnering with

---

60. United Nations, *World Youth Report*.

NGOs and tech hubs, to foster content creation and online safety. Establishing tech fellowships within churches can nurture young tech talents for Kingdom-building through mentorship and collaborative projects. Youth should be supported in using online platforms for advocacy on justice, environmental care, and health, with training in digital campaigning. Churches must recognize and support digital missionaries as vital to their mission. African theological institutions should develop a contextual theology of digital mission, integrating African values and addressing ethical considerations. Empowering digitally fluent and spiritually grounded youth is key to shaping Africa's future with the gospel. In Luke 10:30–37, Jesus tells the well-known parable of the Good Samaritan. A man journeying from Jerusalem to Jericho falls victim to violence – he is attacked, stripped, beaten, and left for dead. A priest, a figure of religious authority and societal hope, walks past without intervening. A Levite, also a revered person in the Jewish society, does the same. But it is the Samaritan – a foreign migrant – who stops, tends to the man's wounds, and pays for his continued care. Jesus concludes by instructing his listeners to "go and do likewise." This story speaks prophetically to the state of many young people across Africa today. Like the wounded man on the roadside, a significant number of African youth find themselves struggling – bruised by poverty, unemployment, violence, poor education systems, climate crises, and neglect from those in power. Many are sidelined in political, economic, and ecclesial spaces. Institutions that should offer hope, such as governments and even the church at times, risk becoming like the priest and the Levite – passing by, unmoved.

Yet, this is precisely where the African church must rediscover its calling as the Good Samaritan. In the immediate term, the church must come alongside young people with practical compassion – offering healing, mentorship, opportunity, and a renewed sense of worth. But this is not enough. In the long term, the church must partner with other stakeholders in transforming the "road from Jerusalem to Jericho" – working toward systems and structures that create safe, just, and enabling environments for all youth. This could mean advocating for education, employment, digital inclusion, environmental stewardship, mental health, and peacebuilding. The future of Africa cannot be imagined apart from its youth. They are not only the leaders of tomorrow but active agents of change today. Their talents, energy, vision, and resilience are indispensable to the continent's development agenda. The church has both a spiritual and civic mandate to equip and empower youth – helping them rise from the roadside and walk boldly toward their God-given destiny. In doing so, the church fulfills not just a humanitarian duty, but a sacred one: nurturing a generation that will shape Africa's future in justice, peace, and flourishing. The harvest is plentiful online, and the workers must no longer remain offline. Now is the time for the church to "go and do likewise."

Discussion Questions

1. In what ways does the large and growing youth population in Africa present both opportunities and challenges for the church and youth ministry?

2. Why should young people be considered central actors in Africa's development agenda, rather than passive beneficiaries?

3. What are the key socio-economic and political challenges limiting youth engagement in development across Africa today?

4. How can the church and youth ministries respond effectively to these challenges in both practical and theological terms?

5. What specific contributions can the church make to foster meaningful youth participation in Africa's development journey?

6. How does empowering youth to lead and own development initiatives contribute to more sustainable and impactful outcomes?

Bibliography

Afifi, Rima. "Youth as Agents of Change." In *Arab Youth: Civic Engagement and Economic Participation*, 8–15. Beirut: UNESCO Regional Bureau, 2011.

Allen, James, Gerald Mohatt, Carlotta Ching Ting Fok, David Henry, and People Awakening Team. "Suicide Prevention as a Community Development Process: Understanding Circumpolar Youth Suicide Prevention through Community Level Outcomes." *International Journal of Circumpolar Health* 68, no. 3 (2009): 274–91.

Anderson, Ray S. *The Shape of Practical Theology: Empowering Ministry with Theological Praxis*. Downers Grove: InterVarsity Press, 2001.

Ansell, Nicola. *Children, Youth and Development*. London: Routledge, 2016.

Autry, Cari E., and Stephen C. Anderson. "Recreation and the Glenview Neighborhood: Implications for Youth and Community Development." *Leisure Sciences* 29, no. 3 (2007): 267–85.

Balcomb, Anthony O. "What Theology? Whose Development? Interrogating Theology and Development in the Secular Academy." *Journal of Theology for Southern Africa* 142 (2012): 6–20.

Balsano, Aida Bilalbegović. "Youth Civic Engagement in the United States: Understanding and Addressing the Impact of Social Impediments on Positive Youth and Community Development." *Applied Developmental Science* 9, no. 4 (2005): 188–201.

Barnett, Rosemary V., and M. A. Brennan. "Integrating Youth into Community Development: Implications for Policy Planning and Program Evaluation." *Journal of Youth Development* 1, no. 2 (2006): 5–19.

Bauman, Zygmunt. "To Hope Is Human." *Tikkun* 19, no. 6 (2004): 64–67.

Becker, Adam B., Jim Randels, and Damian Theodore. "Project BRAVE: Engaging Youth as Agents of Change in a Youth Violence Prevention Project." *Community Youth Development* Special Peer Reviewed Issue (2005): 39–52.

Beukes, Jacques, and Marichen Van der Westhuizen. "Moving from Faith-Based Concerns to Demarginalising Youths through the Circle of Courage." *HTS Teologiese Studies/Theological Studies* 74, no. 3 (2018): 1–9.

Bogenschneider, Karen. "An Ecological Risk/Protective Theory for Building Prevention Programs, Policies, and Community Capacity to Support Youth." *Family Relations* 45 (1996): 127–38.

Boyd, Candice P., Louise Hayes, Rhonda L. Wilson, and Cate Bearsley-Smith. "Harnessing the Social Capital of Rural Communities for Youth Mental Health: An Asset-Based Community Development Framework." *Australian Journal of Rural Health* 16, no. 4 (2008): 189–93.

Bradley, Benjamin Sylvester, Judith Deighton, and Jane Selby. "The 'Voices' Project: Capacity-Building in Community Development for Youth at Risk." *Journal of Health Psychology* 9, no. 2 (2004): 197–212.

Brennan, Mark A. "Conceptualizing Resiliency: An Interactional Perspective for Community and Youth Development." *Child Care in Practice* 14, no. 1 (2008): 55–64.

Brennan, Mark A., and Rosemary V. Barnett. "Bridging Community and Youth Development: Exploring Theory, Research, and Application." *Community Development* 40, no. 4 (2009): 305–10.

Brennan, Mark A., Rosemary V. Barnett, and Brian McGrath. "The Intersection of Youth and Community Development in Ireland and Florida: Building Stronger Communities through Youth Civic Engagement." *Community Development* 40, no. 4 (2009): 331–45.

Brennan, Mark A., Rosemary V. Barnett, and Eboni Baugh. "Youth Involvement in Community Development: Implications and Possibilities for Extension." *The Journal of Extension* 45, no. 4 (2007): 203–13.

Brennan, Mark A., Rosemary V. Barnett, and Marilyn K. Lesmeister. "Enhancing Local Capacity and Youth Involvement in the Community Development Process." *Community Development* 38, no. 4 (2007): 13–27.

Camino, Linda. "Youth-Led Community Building: Promising Practices from Two Communities Using Community-Based Service-Learning." *The Journal of Extension* 43, no. 1 (2005): Article 5.

Campbell, David, and Nancy Erbstein. "Engaging Youth in Community Change: Three Key Implementation Principles." *Community Development* 43, no. 1 (2012): 63–79.

Checkoway, Barry. "What Is Youth Participation?" *Children and Youth Services Review* 33, no. 2 (2011): 340–45.

Checkoway, Barry N., and Lorraine M. Gutierrez. "Youth Participation and Community Change: An Introduction." *Journal of Community Practice* 14, nos. 1–2 (2006): 1–9.

Christens, Brian D., and Tom Dolan. "Interweaving Youth Development, Community Development, and Social Change through Youth Organizing." *Youth & Society* 43, no. 2 (2011): 528–48.

Conner, Jerusha O., and Katherine Cosner. "Youth Change Agents: Comparing the Sociopolitical Identities of Youth Organizers and Youth Commissioners." *Democracy & Education* 24, no. 1 (2016): 1–12.

Delgado, Melvin. *Social Youth Entrepreneurship: The Potential for Youth and Community Transformation*. Westport: Praeger, 2004.

Delgado, Melvin, and Lee Staples. *Youth-Led Community Organizing: Theory and Action*. Oxford: Oxford University Press, 2007.

Demi, Mary Ann, Diane K. McLaughlin, and Anastasia R. Snyder. "Rural Youth Residential Preferences: Understanding the Youth Development-Community Development Nexus." *Community Development* 40, no. 4 (2009): 311–30.

Deneulin, Séverine, and Augusto Zampini Davies. "Theology and Development as Capability Expansion." *HTS: Teologiese Studies/Theological Studies* 72, no. 4 (2016): 1–9.

Fien, John, Cameron Neil, and Matthew Bentley. "Youth Can Lead the Way to Sustainable Consumption." *Journal of Education for Sustainable Development* 2, no. 1 (2008): 51–60.

Filmer, Deon, and Louise Fox. *Youth Employment in Sub-Saharan Africa*. Washington, DC: World Bank, 2014.

Flanagan, Constance A., and Lonnie R. Sherrod. "Youth Political Development: An Introduction." *Journal of Social Issues* 54, no. 3 (1998): 447–56.

Fulford, Stephanie, and Shirley Thompson. "Youth Community Gardening Programming as Community Development: The Youth for EcoAction Program in Winnipeg, Canada." *Canadian Journal of Nonprofit and Social Economy Research* 4, no. 2 (2013): 56–75.

Garcia, Marito, and Jean Fares, eds. *Youth in Africa's Labor Market*. Washington, DC: The World Bank, 2008.

Ginwright, Shawn, and Taj James. "From Assets to Agents of Change: Social Justice, Organizing, and Youth Development." *New Directions for Youth Development* 96 (2002): 27–46.

Heath, Shirley Brice, and Laura Smyth. *ArtShow: Youth and Community Development*. Partners for Livable Communities, 1999.

Ho, Elaine, Amelia Clarke, and Ilona Dougherty. "Youth-Led Social Change: Topics, Engagement Types, Organizational Types, Strategies, and Impacts." *Futures* 67 (2015): 52–62.

Hung, Yvonne. "East New York Farms: Youth Participation in Community Development and Urban Agriculture." *Children, Youth and Environments* 14, no. 1 (2004): 56–85.

International Labour Organization. *Global Employment Trends for Youth 2020: Technology and the Future of Jobs*. Geneva: ILO, 2020.

James, Taj, and Kim McGillicuddy. "Building Youth Movements for Community Change." *Nonprofit Quarterly* 8, no. 4 (2001): 1–3.

Kasumagic, Larisa. "Engaging Youth in Community Development: Post-war Healing and Recovery in Bosnia and Herzegovina." *International Review of Education* 54, no. 3–4 (2008): 375–92.

Makhoul, Jihad, Maysam Alameddine, and Rima A. Afifi. "'I Felt That I Was Benefiting Someone': Youth as Agents of Change in a Refugee Community Project." *Health Education Research* 27, no. 5 (2012): 914–26.

Mandel, Leslie A., and Jasmine Qazilbash. "Youth Voices as Change Agents: Moving beyond the Medical Model in School-Based Health Center Practice." *Journal of School Health* 75, no. 7 (2005): 239–42.

McEvoy-Levy, Siobhan. "Children, Youth and Peacebuilding." In *Critical Issues in Peace and Conflict Studies: Theory, Practice and Pedagogy*, edited by Thomas Matyók, Jessica Senehi, and Sean Byrne, 159–76. Lanham: Lexington Books, 2011.

Mohamed, Inca A., and Wendy Wheeler. "Broadening the Bounds of Youth Development: Youth as Engaged Citizens." Chevy Chase: The Innovation Center for Community and Youth Development, 2001.

National Research Council and Institute of Medicine. *Community Programs to Promote Youth Development*. Edited by Jacquelynne Eccles and Jennifer Appleton Gootman. Washington, DC: National Academies Press, 2002.

Nygreen, Kysa, Soo Ah Kwon, and Patricia Sánchez. "Urban Youth Building Community: Social Change and Participatory Research in Schools, Homes, and Community-Based Organizations." In *Youth Participation and Community Change*, edited by Barry N. Checkoway and Lorraine M. Gutierrez, 107–23. New York: Routledge, 2011.

Pasek, Josh, Kate Kenski, Daniel Romer, and Kathleen Hall Jamieson. "America's Youth and Community Engagement: How Use of Mass Media Is Related to Civic Activity and Political Awareness in 14- to 22-Year-Olds." *Communication Research* 33, no. 3 (2006): 115–35.

Perkins, Daniel F., Lynne M. Borden, Joanne G. Keith, Tianna L. Hoppe-Rooney, and Francisco A. Villarruel. "Community Youth Development." In *Community Youth Development: Programs, Policies, and Practices*, edited by Francisco A. Villarruel, Daniel F. Perkins, Lynne M. Borden, and Joanne G. Keith, 1–23. Thousand Oaks: SAGE, 2003.

Purcell, Rod, and Dave Beck. *Popular Education Practice for Youth and Community Development Work.* Exeter: Learning Matters, 2010.

Schusler, Tania M., and Marianne E. Krasny. "Environmental Action as Context for Youth Development." *The Journal of Environmental Education* 41, no. 4 (2010): 208–23.

Schwartz, Stephanie. *Youth and Post-Conflict Reconstruction: Agents of Change.* Washington, DC: United States Institute of Peace Press, 2010.

Soleimanpour, S., C. Brindis, S. Geierstanger, S. Kandawalla, and T. Kurlaender. "Incorporating Youth-Led Community Participatory Research into School Health Center Programs and Policies." *Public Health Reports* 123, no. 6 (2008): 709–716.

Sommers, Marc. "Urban Youth in Africa." *Environment and Urbanization* 22, no. 2 (2010): 317–32.

Sutton, Sharon Egretta. "A Social Justice Perspective on Youth and Community Development: Theorizing the Processes and Outcomes of Participation." *Children, Youth and Environments* 17, no. 2 (2007): 616–45.

Teague, Karee. "Agents of Change: Thoughts on Youth Development." *Journal of Extension* 39, no. 3 (2001): 53–56.

Tolman, Joel, Karen Pittman, Barbara Cervone, Kathleen Cushman, Lisa Rowley, Sheila Kinkade, Jeanie Phillips, and Sabrina Duque. "Youth Acts, Community Impacts: Stories of Youth Engagement with Real Results." Community & Youth Development Series, Volume 7. Takoma Park: Forum for Youth Investment, 2001.

United Nations. *Recover Better: Economic and Social Challenges and Opportunities.* New York: United Nations, 2020.

———. *World Youth Report: Youth, Social Entrepreneurship and the 2030 Agenda.* New York: United Nations, 2020.

Valaitis, Ruta K. "Computers and the Internet: Tools for Youth Empowerment." *Journal of Medical Internet Research* 7, no. 5 (2005): e433.

Weber, Shantelle. "Decolonising Youth Ministry Models? Challenges and Opportunities in Africa." *HTS: Teologiese Studies/Theological Studies* 73, no. 4 (2017): 1–10.

Weissman, Harold H. *Community Development in the Mobilization for Youth Experience.* New York: Association Press, 1969.

Wheaton, Belinda, Georgina Roy, and Rebecca Olive. "Exploring Critical Alternatives for Youth Development through Lifestyle Sport: Surfing and Community Development in Aotearoa/New Zealand." *Sustainability* 9, no. 12 (2017): 2298.

World Bank. *End Extreme Poverty and Promote Shared Prosperity.* New York: World Bank, 2013.

Yohalem, Nicole, and Shanetta Martin. "Building the Evidence Base for Youth Engagement: Reflections on Youth and Democracy." *Journal of Community Psychology* 35, no. 6 (2007): 807–10.

Youniss, James, and Heinz Reinders. "Youth and Community Service: A Review of US Research, a Theoretical Perspective, and Implications for Policy in Germany." *Zeitschrift für Erziehungswissenschaft* 13, no. 2 (2010): 233–48.

Youniss, James, and Miranda Yates. *Community Service and Social Responsibility in Youth*. Chicago: University of Chicago Press, 1997.

Zeldin, Shepherd. "Youth as Agents of Adult and Community Development: Mapping the Processes and Outcomes of Youth Engaged in Organizational Governance." *Applied Developmental Science* 8, no. 2 (2004): 75–90.

Zeldin, Shepherd, Brian D. Christens, and Jane L. Powers. "The Psychology and Practice of Youth-Adult Partnership: Bridging Generations for Youth Development and Community Change." *American Journal of Community Psychology* 51 (2013): 385–97.

Zeldin, Shepherd, Linda Camino, and Matthew Calvert. "Toward an Understanding of Youth in Community Governance: Policy Priorities and Research Directions." *Social Policy Report*. Volume 17, Number 3 Society for Research in Child Development (2003).

6

Creating a Digital Environment on Social Media for Self-Identity Formation

Ogidi Joshua Dickson

This chapter[1] examines how young people's "interface" with social media shapes their self-identity formation as they engage with other social media users. The chapter focuses on the potency of social media in creating a digital environment where young people interact and share both censored and uncensored information. Social media refers to digital technological media that create a digital environment for networking between users who interface and share information with each other. Social media serves as a digital environment that creates platforms for disseminating information that plays a key role in shaping the self-identity of young people.

Data was gathered from existing literature and analysed through conceptual analysis to investigate the question "How does young people's interface or engagement with social media influence their self-identity formation?" In addressing this question, I employed conceptual analysis to conceptualize social media, self-identity formation, and how young people's interface or engagement on social media influences their self-identity formation.

This chapter argues from a theological perspective that self-identity is both discovered and developed; it is discovered by viewing self-identity through a Christian lens and developed through an interdisciplinary dialogue with Erik Erikson's psychosocial development stages of human engagement with

---

1. This chapter is derived from the researcher's MTh thesis at Stellenbosch University, South Africa.

social institutions like social media. These findings reveal that social media has become part and parcel of young people's daily lives, influencing them in areas such as impression management, self-disclosure, self-identification, and even character assassination.

Key words: social media, self-identity formation, impression management, psychosocial development theory.

Introduction

Social media creates a digital environment that is an integral part of everyday life. Qualman argues that the understanding of the usage and influence of social media is a fundamental, because social media usage is an integral part of humanity's experience of daily living.[2] Social media and its influence are embedded in our daily interactions. This introduction outlines the research focus of this chapter and describes its focus as it addresses the question "How does young people's interface or engagement[3] on social media influence their self-identity formation?" Theologically, self-identity formation – in relation to both the concept and the praxis – is discovered and developed within the framework of Christian identity.

Engaging with Erik Erikson's psychosocial development theory, I discovered that self-identity formation develops through interface with various social institutions such as family, educational institutions, and social media. This chapter focuses on the social institution of social media because the research question in view aims to examine how social media influences young people's self-identity formation. In examining how social media influences young peo-

---

2. Qualman, *Socialnomics*, 262.

3. Interface is the networking point where social media users "meet" or connect on a device or an app to participate in shared interests. It connotes the interaction between two or more people on a digital platform. Capurro, "Ethical Issues," 162; Osatuyi, "Information Sharing," 2622. Interface could also refer to the user's interaction with a device or an app. Dijck, *Culture of Connectivity*, 10. In this research study, the term "interface" denotes people's interaction with other users and with disseminated content (information) shared on social media.

ple's self-identity formation, I utilized two of Erikson's eight stages of psycho-social development[4] – the fifth and sixth stages.[5]

These two stages suggest that within the age range of eighteen to thirty-five, young people's self-identity can be developed and shaped. This understanding suggests that the self-identity formation of young people in Nigeria, Africa, and worldwide is developed, and can be influenced – negatively or positively.

Methodology

The methodology of a research study, which is fundamental to how the research is conducted, involves a process, tools, and procedures to examine the research topic.[6] With regard to this chapter, the research is qualitative in nature and the methodology used is conceptual analysis. According to both Mouton and Du Plooy-Cilliers, conceptual analysis provides theoretical clarity by engaging with the literature of academic discourse and scholarly reviews.[7]

By utilizing conceptual analysis, the researcher clarifies meanings and defines the concept and praxis of social media, self-identity formation, and other terminologies that are contextual to this research by engaging ongoing academic conversation and scholarship through journals, newsletters, authors, experts and researchers. In summary, conceptual analysis provides clarity to subjects and phenomena that may be interconnected – for example, investigating how social media influences the self-identity formation of young people. However, a weakness of conceptual analysis is that concepts are sometimes poorly constructed, leading to conceptual confusion, theoretical ambiguities, and flawed reasoning.[8] This chapter addresses this weakness by following

---

4. Erikson developed an eight (8) psychosocial development stage theory. Categorized based on age. These stages are as follows: Trust vs Mistrust (0–1 year), Autonomy vs Shame (1–3 years), Initiative vs Guilt (3–6 years), Industry (competence) vs Inferiority (6–12 years), Identity vs Role confusion (12–18 years), Intimacy vs Isolation (18–40 years), Generativity vs Stagnation (40–65 years), Ego integrity vs Despair (65 years and above). Of these eight stages, Identity vs Role confusion (12–18 years) and Intimacy vs Isolation (18–40 years) are particularly relevant to this chapter because the age ranges of these stages align with the age categorization of young people in Nigeria, where youth are classified as those between the ages of eighteen to thirty-five. Badejo, Stephens, and Anyanwu, "Counselling Needs," 284; Ogidi, "Social Media," 10.

5. Erikson's fifth stage of psychosocial development describes how young people between ages twelve and eighteen seek to understand their roles and identity. Similarly, Erikson's sixth stage deals with young people between the ages of eighteen and forty who grabble with the issues of of intimacy versus isolation.

6. Hansen, "Method and Methodology"; Mouton, *How to Succeed*, 57.

7. Mouton, 87, 175;

8. Mouton, 177.

Huysamen's recommendation to remain focused on the methodology chosen when reviewing the published scholarly literature on a particular topic.[9] This ensures that the research identifies inconsistencies and gaps that may justify further research on aspects of social media's influence on young people's self-idcntity formation.

Conceptualization of Components

This section conceptualizes the two components of this chapter: social media and self-identity formation. A conceptual understanding of these components helps address the problem of how young people's interface with social media influences their self-identity formation.

Social Media

Different disciplines understand social media differently, and these varying views about social media inform and shape their interface with users on social media. From a telecommunications perspective, Marwick and Ellison see social networking sites like Facebook as platforms for public displays of connection and expression of emotions and opinions.[10] O'Reilly and Milstein view social media as both a professional and personal medium for expressing users' identities on social networking sites.[11] Cloete, adopting a theological perspective conceptualizes social media as a digital culture and space (environment) for young people.[12]

In addition, social media is a digital environment for interface between social media users. Social media are technological media that create digital environments that serve as information and web-based services that allow individuals and corporations to construct their public and private identities.[13]

Moreover, users engage with social media on different platforms such as social networking sites – to share information and connect with offline and online friends – wikis – to share, modify, create, and disseminate information – and blogs – to create content and interface with network followers. These platforms disseminate information that influences young people's self-identity

9. Huysamen, *Methodology*, 190.
10. Marwick and Ellison, "There Isn't WiFi in Heaven!," 378.
11. O'Reilly and Milstein, *Twitter Book*, 169.
12. Cloete, "Digital Culture," 1; Cloete, "Youth Culture," 2.
13. Boyd and Ellison, "Social Network Sites," 211; Qualman, *Socialnomics*, 64.

formation. The information shared creates a digital environment filled with uncensored information that can be used for a variety of purposes. As young people engage with the social media space, this uncensored information can influence them in their self-identity formation.

Self-Identity Formation

Ndubisi defines self-identity as the "distinguishing characteristics of a person or being."[14] Self-identity formation involves understanding and discovering the unique qualities that make up a person. Self-identity refers to the qualities that distinguish a person from other people and also includes how a person desires to be identified.

Self-identity formation is (i) discovered through a Christian identity[15] and (ii) developmentally constructed in stages.[16] This chapter theologically conceptualizes self-identity formation as both a Christian identity and a process consisting of several developmental stages. In examining how self-identity is developed and constructed, this chapter utilizes the fifth and sixth stages of Erikson's psychosocial development theory.

(i) Self-identity formation: Christian identity

Based on the *National Study of Youth and Religion*, Dean observes that young people sometimes separate their relationship with God from their identity formation.[17] She argues that even those born and raised in Christian families and Christian communities may not experience a nurturing connection with God in the formation of their Christian identity. Elton emphasizes that youth ministry leaders should guide young people in developing their Christian identity and argues that:

> if ministry leaders are to help nurture their identity as children of God and help them discover a faith that speaks into the current culture, it will be important to help them shift from viewing them-

---

14. Ndubisi, *The Philosophical Paradigm of African Identity and Development*, 222. Belanger, *Merriam-Webster's*, 933; Black et al., *Collins English Dictionary*, 1487.

15. The discovery of self-identity entails an understanding of humanity as a creation of God, created for his purpose and mission.

16. The developed and constructed self-identity involves young people going through different phases of life that shape their self-identity formation. These different phases are influenced by different social institutions such as social media.

17. Dean, *Almost Christian*, 16.

selves as objects within a consumer society to seeing themselves as subjects and agents of God's love.[18]

Jacober, who discusses identity within the context of Christian youth, submits that identity is something that young people discover and create by telling their stories to themselves and others on their social media space.[19] This suggests that a young person's identity is both discovered and developed. Identity as discovered means that young people understand themselves as the humans beings whom God says they are.[20] Identity as developed means that young people's identity is influenced by other factors such as family upbringing, the environment in which they were raised, and the friends they connect with on social media.

Jacober further stresses that Christian young people need to understand identity theories and philosophical perspectives of "self-autonomy" in order to develop their identity.[21] However, in the development of identity, the theology of God's creation and the significance of participating in the suffering of Jesus death and resurrection influences the self-identity of young people.[22]

Strommen and Hardel argue that Christian families inform and influence young people's Christian identity and emphasize that Christian families must create and promote a healthy Christian atmosphere for children and youth, where healthy behaviours characterized by love, care, and integrity are the normal daily way of life.[23] Experiencing unhealthy behaviours in one's family of origin – for example, wounded memories, hurtful recollections, unmet personal needs, unfulfilled ambitions, and feelings of failure – can adversely impact young people's Christian identity and their disposition towards the Christian faith. It is important to address such unhealthy behaviours and promote parental harmony.

Therefore, Christian youth should understand identity from a holistic perspective, seeing it as both discovered – as designed by God – and developed through the influence of family, society, and social media.[24] Elton emphasizes that Christian young people should understand their identity as children of

---

18. Elton, "Story," 168.
19. Jacober, "Adolescent Identity Development," 97.
20. Jacober, 100.
21. Jacober, 100.
22. Jacober, 101.
23. Strommen and Hardel, *Passing On the Faith*, 38.
24. Jacober, "Adolescent Identity Development," 105.

God, who are both God's subjects and his agents of change.[25] As both Jacober and Elton argue, while the self-identity of Christian youth is influenced by parents, families, society, and social media, their primary understanding of identity should be rooted in their identity as God's subjects and his agents of change in society.[26]

(ii) Self-identity as developed: Erikson's psychosocial development theory

In his psychosocial development theory, psychologist Erik Erikson outlines eight stages of human development that influence self-identity formation. These eight stages are as follows: Trust vs Mistrust (0–1 year),[27] Autonomy vs Shame (1–3 years),[28] Initiative vs Guilt (3–6 years),[29] Industry (competence) vs Inferiority (6–12 years),[30] Identity vs Role Confusion (12–18 years),[31] Intimacy vs Isolation (18–40 years),[32] Generativity vs Stagnation (40–65 years),[33] and Ego Integrity vs Despair (65 years and above).[34] Interacting with Erikson's fifth and sixth stages shows how young people's identity development is influenced by various social institutions, including social media. I will discuss these two developmental stages as propounded by Erikson and how they are particularly vulnerable to external influences.

---

25. Elton, "Story," 171.

26. Jacober, "Adolescent Identity Development," 106; Elton, "Story," 171.

27. For further reading, see Erikson, *Identity, Youth and Crisis*, 96; Erikson, "Psychoanalysis," 193; Erikson, "Eight Stages of Man," 67; Williams, "Shame and Anxiety," 2; Ogidi, "Social Media," 61–62.

28. For further reading, see Erikson, *Identity, Youth and Crisis*, 110; Erikson, "Psychoanalysis," 194; Erikson, "Eight Stages of Man," 67; Williams, "Shame and Anxiety," 2; Ogidi, "Social Media," 63.

29. For further reading, see Erikson, *Identity, Youth and Crisis*, 96, 116, 121; Erikson, "Psychoanalysis," 195; Ogidi, "Social Media," 64.

30. For further reading, see Erikson, *Identity, Youth and Crisis*, 122–25; McLeod, "Erik Erikson," np; Williams, "Shame and Anxiety," 2; Ogidi, "Social Media," 65.

31. For further reading, see Erikson, *Identity, Youth and Crisis*, 128–29; Williams, "Shame and Anxiety," 3; Ogidi, "Social Media," 65.

32. For further reading, see Erikson, *Identity, Youth and Crisis*, 135; Williams, "Shame and Anxiety," 2; Ogidi, "Social Media," 66–67.

33. For further reading, see Erikson, *Identity, Youth and Crisis*, 138–39; Ogidi, "Social Media," 67.

34. For further reading, see Erikson, *Identity, Youth and Crisis*, 140; McLeod, "Erik Erikson," np; Ogidi, "Social Media," 68.

Fifth Stage: Identity vs. Role Confusion (12–18 Years)

The fifth stage of identity formation takes place between the ages of twelve and eighteen years. The basic virtue sought by an adolescent at this stage is fidelity and curiosity.[35] Erikson and Williams contend that children become more will-driven, independent, purposeful, and competent, and begin to imagine, understand, and interpret the world based on their own experiences.[36] During this stage, the adolescent becomes role-driven. They want to act out roles that express their identity and influence the way others identify them.[37] They play these roles with their parents, family members, and friends, and even in their career choices, seeking to be identified as individuals and as members of certain groups in society.

Jordán-Conde, Mennecke, and Townsend note that during this period, adolescents explore possibilities and begin to form their own identities based on the outcome of their explorations.[38] They begin to create a mental picture of the occupation with which they want to be identified. Erikson posits that the search for identity has the potential to create an identity crisis if adolescents experience "set-backs" failure during process of exploration.[39] McLeod explains that failure to establish a sense of identity in society ("I don't know what I want to be when I grow up") can lead to role confusion.[40] This confusion takes place when individuals are not being sure about themselves or their place in society. Erikson explains that in response to this role confusion or identity crisis, adolescents may begin to experiment with different lifestyles in imitation of others.[41]

The experiences of young people within a particular age group are not universal and the environment in which they are nurtured significantly influences the developmental stages that they experience.

Sixth Stage: Intimacy vs. Isolation (18–40 Years)

The sixth stage of identity formation takes place between the ages of eighteen and forty years, and the psychosocial crisis that characterizes this stage is inti-

---

35. Erikson, *Identity, Youth and Crisis*, 128.
36. Erikson, 189; Williams, "Shame and Anxiety," 3.
37. McLeod, "Erik Erikson," np.
38. Jordán-Conde, Mennecke, and Townsend, "Late Adolescent Identity Definition," 354.
39. Erikson, *Identity, Youth and Crisis*, 134.
40. McLeod, "Erik Erikson," np.
41. Erikson, *Identity, Youth and Crisis*, 129.

macy versus isolation.[42] The basic virtue sought by a person at this stage is love. During this stage, young people develop a fair idea of their desired occupation (career) and are more concerned about establishing relationships that will be helpful and meaningful in their career decisions, marriage, and social identity.[43]

Young people establish relationships with those whom they love, as well as with those they know or believe love them. Erikson explains that at this stage, young people tend to be reciprocal in expressing their love.[44] For example, they tend to reciprocate the love their parents showed them when they were growing up, and they also show love to people they do not know but who seems to understand them. This tendency exposes young people to various influences that may lead to either constructive or destructive constructions of their identities.

Influence of Social Media in African Society

Essoungou, an African social media scholar, argues that with the invention of mobile phones in the mid-1990s, over four hundred million Africans have subscribed to mobile phone usage.[45] This practice became the bedrock for the spread of social media in Africa. Essoungou also asserts that for an African, social media is a tool and platform for interaction among users,[46] with social media sites like Facebook launching versions in major African languages like Swahili, Hausa, and Zulu. Similarly, Bohler-Muller and Merwe, who are also African scholars, say that social media is a digital environment that is used to influence the sociopolitical experience in Africa.[47] For example, the 2010–2011 revolutions against tyrannical governance in Tunisia and Egypt were organized and driven through social media, which allowed users to interact and engage with one another in a digital environment and unite in their call for democratically elected governments. Both Essoungou and Bohler-Muller and Merwe – who explore different usage of social media and its influence in Africa note that (1) Africans are heavy users on social media for different purposes,

42. Erikson, 135; Williams, "Shame and Anxiety," 2; Ogidi, "Social Media," 67.

43. Jordán-Conde, Mennecke, and Townsend, "Late Adolescent Identity Definition," 356; McLeod, "Erik Erikson," np.

44. Erikson, *Identity, Youth and Crisis*, 137.

45. Essoungou, "Social Media Boom," 1.

46. Essoungou, 1.

47. Bohler-Muller and Van der Merwe, "Potential of Social Media," 1.

(2) social media significantly influences Africans, and (3) it is a platform for social engagement and interaction among users in a digital environment.[48]

In Nigeria, social media is redefining self-identity formation among young people between the ages eighteen and thirty-five years. Nkechi and Christian, who are both Nigerian scholars, conducted empirical research on the engagement – that is, the accessing and disseminating of information – of Nigerian youth on social media. They argue that social media is a fascinating technological medium of interaction and engagement among young people who interact with each other as social media users.[49] Their empirical research findings reveal that Nigerian youth are very likely to use social media as a medium of interaction and socialization with friends, family, and society.[50]

Furthermore, Nkechi and Christian argue that young people's engagement on social media influences their identities, especially how they perceive themselves and how they want other people to perceive them in the digital environment. Oso – who is also a Nigerian – reasons that social media greatly influences Nigerian youth, to the extent that in 2013, the Federal Government sought to impose restrictions and monitor social media interactions in order to censor information dissemination.[51] Although not implemented, the desire to impose such measures reflects the concerns about the influence of social media on the youth of Nigeria.[52]

Influence of Social Media on Self-Identity Formation

Social media provides young people with a public interactive space for engagement with friends and potential friends. Jacober reasons that social media is viewed by some as a new mall, town square, or public sphere, where young people gather to impact and influences one another's self-identity formation and development.[53] These new digital spaces, where young people establish both online and offline friendships, offer arenas and locations for them to

48. Essoungou, "Social Media Boom," 1; Bohler-Muller and Van der Merwe, "Potential of Social Media," 1.

49. Nkechi and Christian, "Moral Implication," 2232.

50. Nkechi and Christian, 2232; Ogidi, "Social Media," 40.

51. Oso, "Media and Democracy," 13.

52. Pursuant to this chapter, further research could involve conducting an empirical study on how social media is influencing self-identity formation among young people in of Nigeria. This study could focus on young people in cosmopolitan cities or rural area, or it could seek to discover how social media influences young people's spirituality.

53. Jacober, "Adolescent Identity Development," 105.

converge and develop their identities. With the rapid rise of social media and other information and communication technologies, the concept of the town square or public sphere for interaction and networking has expanded beyond a mere geographical location and become a global and boundless space. Therefore, the public's influence on young people's identity formation is now global, extending beyond their parents, family members, and immediate society.

The social media apps that young people download and use often reflect their self-identity. Gardner and Davis suggest that the app icons that young people download from social media on their technological devices offer clues about identity because these icons represent what the young person finds desirable.[54] They give a unique insight into their interest. The apps that young people frequently access and devote their time to are indicators of who they are and how they want to be perceived.

Strommen and Hardel argue that "media that encourages self-gratification, individualism, anti-authoritarianism, and the like are powerful shapers of the attitudes and values not only of young people but also of families, communities, and the culture itself."[55] Some of the individualistic gratifications and aspects of self-identity formation on social media are conceptualized below.

Impression management

According to Boyd and Ellison and Ogidi, impression management on social media refers to how young people present a profile picture or data about themselves that may be inconsistent with their real selves.[56] This involves creating an image or sharing information about oneself that is not true but is intended to impress other network users. This discrepancy between their real selves and their profile images could be as a result of what MacKinnon and Heise term "a demanded identity." A demanded identity is an identity that is demanded by a particular social environment or social institution.[57]

Self-disclosure

Media psychologists Tsay-Vogel and Oliver agree that social media aids self-disclosure among users[58] because self-disclosure is a process in which personal and private information is shared and becomes public knowledge – which

---

54. Gardner and Davis, *App Generation*, 60.

55. Strommen and Hardel, *Passing On the Faith*, 257.

56. Boyd and Ellison, 220; Ogidi, "Social Media," 19.

57. MacKinnon and Heise, "Self, Identity, and Social Institutions," 466.

58. Tsay-Vogel and Oliver, "Is Watching Others," 112.

means that the information disclosed on social media becomes publicly accessible. Young people often share and make public personal and private information. From a youth ministry standpoint, Allison concurs and affirms that young people share their personal and private information with other young people in their networks on social media.[59] Such self-disclosure on social media fosters closeness, friendship, familiarity, and satisfaction through interaction.

Tsay-Vogel and Oliver confirm that self-disclosure on social media helps people to feel connected to each other, enhancing closeness and dyadic interactions despite geographical distance. Boyd and Ellison offer a perspective on self-disclosure. In contrast to Tsay-Vogel and Oliver's view that self-disclosure is a means of connecting young people, Boyd and Ellison prefer the term "self-presentation" arguing that some young people only present certain aspects of themselves on social media, which may not be an accurate profile of who they really are.[60]

The self-disclosure of users on social media contributes to the formation of youth culture. Allison claims that since social media provides young people with a platform to disclose their identities, ideologies, and daily event updates, this contributes to the formation of a shared youth culture of communication among generational peers across the globe.[61] This youth culture is given various names by different scholars. Theologian Walt Mueller calls it "the audiovideo generation," "the cyberkids generation," or "the digital age generation."[62] Mueller argues that the diversity of ways in which young people are using digital media to create youth culture are causing both anxiety and optimism in youth ministry.[63] The reason for these mixed feelings is the fact that self-disclosure on social media creates a commonality of depersonalized identities, ideologies, language, and culture that is unique to peers, their generation, and some social media followers.

Sharing of content

Social media creates a digital environment that is conducive to constructive Christian identity formation. In Jacober's opinion, young people's self-identity is influenced by shared stories.[64] Social media affords young people opportu-

---

59. Allison, "Youth," 69.
60. Boyd and Ellison, "Social Network Sites," 220.
61. Allison, "Youth," 69.
62. Mueller, *Youth Culture 101*, 2.
63. Mueller, 2.
64. Jacober, "Adolescent Identity, Development," 97.

nities to share their stories, which can influence other users' perceptions of themselves. Jacober also suggests that young people create identities by telling and re-telling their stories among themselves and to others within their social circles.[65] Thus, sharing stories on social media can encourage social media users to create a Christian identity. This is possible by sharing stories about Bible characters and personal experience on social media in ways that promote narratives of deeper understanding of God. Such stories reveal their Christian identity – that is, who God says they are.

Self-identification

Tsay-Vogel and Oliver, arguing from the point of view of the entertainment industry, note that societal celebrities on social media use character perception to influence the self-identity of their network of followers.[66] Self-disclosure by such celebrities influences their audience's self-identity and character. Deacy and Arweck reason that social media influences self-identity formation and argue that since the internet provides a space in which identity is being worked out, and since social media and the internet are inseparable, the identities of a large population are influenced through interactions on social media plat-forms.[67] In this context, societal celebrities feature prominently in various areas of social interests among young people, such as music, movies, comedy, and sports.

Gossip and character assassination

Social media facilitates gossip, character assassination, and the spread of rumours. Boyd argues that gossip seems to take on a new dimension on social media.[68] It facilitates a new dimension on social media because it enables people to share content and information about other people, which may or may not be true. For example, he points out that a rumour shared on Facebook by a mischievous person has the potential to quickly spread to millions of users.[69]

However, Boyd also notes that it is not Facebook itself, as a social media network, that creates gossip or assassinates character but, rather, the social media network users who interface on Facebook. Social media users reveal

---

65. Jacober, 97.

66. Tsay-Vogel and Oliver, "Is Watching Others," 112; Ogidi, "Social Media," 17.

67. Deacy and Arweck, *Exploring Religion*, 238.

68. Boyd, *It's Complicated*, 145.

69. Boyd, 145.

their identities through their engagement with other network users, leveraging available platforms to share information or stories.

Conclusion

According to Qualman, social media has become part and parcel of daily living. Therefore, we do not have a choice as regards the existence of social media and its influence; rather, our concern must be with how we use social media and harness its ability to influence to serve humanity.[70] Erikson's psychosocial theory of developmental stages of humanity depicts that the self-identity formation of young people is developed and constructed through engagement with different social institutions like social media.

Erikson's psychosocial theory of identity formation in conversation with biblical understanding of identity formation depicts an interdisciplinary discourse on the subject of self, identity, identity formation, and the role that social media plays in influencing young people's self-identity formation. Also, due to young people's interface with network users on social media as a digital environment, their self-identity formation is vulnerable to certain construct and identities like impression management, self-disclosure, self-identification, rumour spreading and character assassination.

Discussion Questions

1. How can you create a digital environment on social media?

2. What is the importance of creating a digital environment on social media.

3. In what ways does social media influence young people's self-identity formation?

4. How can young people positively influence social media users with their Christian identity?

5. Why is it crucial to help young people during the fifth and sixth stages of Erik Erikson's psychosocial theory?

---

70. Qualman, *Socialnomics*, 262.

Bibliography

Allison, Sheila. "Youth and the (Potential) Power of Social Media." *Youth Studies Australia* 32, no. 3 (2013): 69–73.

Badejo, A. O., O. A. Stephens, and A. C. Anyanwu. "A Study of the Counselling Needs of Nigerian Youths in the Current Political Dispensation." *Journal of Emerging Trends in Educational Research and Policy Studies* 2, no. 4 (2011): 284–89.

Belanger, M. *Merriam-Webster's Collegiate Thesaurus*. 2nd ed. Springfield: Merriam-Webster, 2010.

Black, D., I. Brookes, R. Groves, A. Holmes, H. Hucker, C. McKeown, and E. Summers. *Collins English Dictionary*. Glasgow: HarperCollins, 2009.

Bohler-Muller, Narnia, and Charl Van der Merwe. "The Potential of Social Media to Influence Socio-Political Change on the African Continent." Africa Institute of South Africa, Policy Brief 46, no. 2 (2011).

Boyd, Danah. *It's Complicated: The Social Lives of Networked Teens*. New Haven: Yale University Press, 2014.

Boyd, Danah M., and Nicole B. Ellison. "Social Network Sites: Definition, History, and Scholarship." *Journal of Computer-Mediated Communication* 13, no. 1 (2007): 210–30.

Capurro, Rafael. "Ethical Issues of Online Social Networks in Africa." *Innovation* 47 (2013): 160–74.

Castells, Manuel. *The Power of Identity*. New York: Wiley & Sons, 2011.

Cloete, Anita L. "Living in a Digital Culture: The Need for Theological Reflection." *HTS Teologiese Studies/Theological Studies* 71, no. 2 (2015): 1–7.

———. "Youth Culture, Media and Sexuality: What Could Faith Communities Contribute?" *HTS Teologiese Studies/Theological Studies* 68, no. 2 (2012): 1–8.

Deacy, Christopher, and Elisabeth Arweck, eds. *Exploring Religion and the Sacred in a Media Age*. Farnham: Ashgate, 2009.

Dean, Kenda C. *Almost Christian: What the Faith of Our Teenagers Is Telling the American Church*. New York: Oxford University Press, 2010.

Dijck, Jose van. *The Culture of Connectivity: A Critical History of Social Media*. New York: Oxford University Press, 2013.

Elton, Terri L. "The Story We Find Ourselves In: Nurturing Christian Identity in a Consumer Culture." *Word & World* 34, no. 2 (2014): 168–77.

Erikson, Erik H. "Eight Stages of Man." In *Personality: Critical Concepts in Psychology*, edited by C. L. Cooper and Lawrence A. Pervin. New York: Routledge, 1998.

———. *Identity, Youth and Crisis*. New York: Norton, 1968.

———. "Psychoanalysis and the Life Cycle." In *Personality Theories: An Introduction*, edited by B. Engler, 185–213. Boston: Houghton Mifflin, 1985.

Essoungou, A. "A Social Media Boom Begins in Africa: Using Mobile Phones." *African Renewal* 24 (2010): 3–4.

Gardner, Howard, and Katie Davis. *The App Generation: How Today's Youth Navigate Identity, Intimacy, and Imagination in a Digital World.* Yale University Press, 2013.

Hansen, L. "Method and Methodology." Lecture presented at the Faculty of Theology, Stellenbosch University, 2014.

Huysamen, G. K. *Methodology for the Social and Behavioural Sciences.* Halfway House, Johannesburg: Southern Book Publishers, 1994.

Jacober, A. "Adolescent Identity Development." In *Christian Youth Work in Theory and Practice,* edited by S. Nash and J. Whitehead, 97–112. London: SCM, 2014.

"Join the Global Conversation" (2010). https://read.un-ilibrary.org/economic-and-social-development/a-social-media-boom-begins-in-africa_ff4217a4-en#page1. Accessed 5 August 2020.

Jordán-Conde, Zayira, Brian Mennecke, and Anthony Townsend. "Late Adolescent Identity Definition and Intimate Disclosure on Facebook." *Computers in Human Behavior* 33 (2014): 356–66.

MacKinnon, N. J. and Heise, D. R. "Self, Identity, and Social Institutions." *Contemporary Sociology A Journal of Reviews* 40, no. 4 (2011): 465–67.

Marwick, Alice, and Nicole B. Ellison. "'There Isn't WiFi in Heaven!' Negotiating Visibility on Facebook Memorial Pages." *Journal of Broadcasting & Electronic Media* 56, no. 3 (2012): 378–400.

McLeod, Saul. "Erik Erikson's Stages of Psychosocial Development." *Simply Psychology,* updated 25 January 2024. https://www.simplypsychology.org/erik-erikson.html. Accessed 22 April 2015.

Mouton, Johann. *How to Succeed in Your Master's and Doctoral Studies: A South African Guide and Resource Book.* Pretoria: Van Schaik, 2001.

Mueller, W. *Youth Culture 101.* Grand Rapid: Zondervan, 2007.

Ndubisi, F. O. 2013. "The Philosophical Paradigm of African Identity and Development." *Open Journal of Philosophy* 3, no.1A (2013): 222–30.

Nkechi, O., and N. G. Christian. "The Moral Implication of Social Media Phenomenon in Nigeria." *Mediterranean Journal of Social Sciences* 5, no. 20 (2014): 2231–37.

Ogidi, Joshua Dickson. "Social Media as a Source of Self-Identity Formation: Challenges and Opportunities for Youth Ministry." MTh thesis, Stellenbosch University, 2015. http://scholar.sun.ac.za.

O'Reilly, Tim, and Sarah Milstein. *The Twitter Book.* Sebastopol: O'Reilly Media, 2009.

Osatuyi, Babajide. "Information Sharing on Social Media Sites." *Computers in Human Behavior* 29, no. 6 (2013): 2622–31.

Oso, L. "Media and Democracy in Nigeria: A Critique of Liberal Perspective." *New Media and Mass Communication* 10 (2013): 13–22.

Qualman, Erik. *Socialnomics: How Social Media Transforms the Way We Live and Do Business.* Hoboken: Wiley & Sons, 2011.

Strommen, Merton P., and Richard A. Hardel. *Passing On the Faith: A Radical New Model for Youth and Family Ministry.* Winona: St. Mary's Press, 2000.

Tsay-Vogel, Mina, and Mary Beth Oliver. "Is Watching Others Self-Disclose Enjoyable? An Examination of the Effects of Information Delivery in Entertainment Media." *Journal of Psychology* 26, no. 3 (2014): 111–24.

Williams, L. "Shame and Anxiety in Counselling the Youth," Christian Youth Forum on Youth Identity Crisis: Finding God without Losing Self. Seminar held at Stellenbosch University, 24 April 2015.

7

Youth and Social Justice

Nathan H. Chiroma

Introduction

The role of young people in advocating for social justice cannot be overemphasized. Recent trends in Africa – such as #FeesMustFall in South Africa, the Arab Uprisings in North Africa, #EndSARS in Nigeria, and #RejectFinanceBill2024 in Kenya[1] – highlight the significant role young people play in the quest for social justice. Similarly, in other parts of the world such as America, the emergence of Black Lives Matter, championed by young people in the quest for justice against police brutality, highlights the role of young people in the quest for social justice. Until recent times, social justice has often been an untravelled road for youth because young people themselves are frequently identified as the problem. They are often perceived as lacking the ability to engage in social justice because they, just like unjust systems, need to be changed. Kelly notes that although youth are more likely to face many problems in life because they are vulnerable to youthful folly and tend to act unwisely and without restraint, it is wrong for people to define them as problems.[2] He goes on to add that the challenges and problems that young people face are not unique and that adults of all ages are certainly vulnerable to such problems. Therefore, we need to separate our understanding of youth from unjust systems of oppression and recognize that young people are often victims of these systems. Hence, instead of victimizing these young people, we need to refocus our minds and address the oppressive environments they

---

1. These are youth-led actions against various governments in light of social justice.
2. Kelly, "Theology of Youth Ministry," 17.

live in. By doing so, we can help them to confront the problems they face and empower them to partake in the global fight for social justice.

Defying the belief that they are a problem requiring resolution, it is noteworthy that young people have consistently demonstrated their ability to actively participate in the pursuit of social justice despite facing many obstacles. Traditionally, they have engaged in social movements and played important roles in correcting socio-economic disparities. Therefore, when provided with the opportunity, young people possess the ability to assume important responsibilities in the pursuit of social justice. Hence, this chapter aims to explain the various roles that young individuals assume in the pursuit of social justice. Advocating for social fairness yields advantages for all individuals. Any form of injustice poses a danger to justice in all places. Every individual's human dignity must be respected and maintained.

Definitions of Terms

Both youth and social justice are abstract ideas that carry distinct connotations, meanings, and assumptions. To ensure clarity, this study will explain the significance of these terms and demonstrate their application.

Youth

Attempting to encapsulate the concept of youth lucidly and succinctly can frequently prove challenging due to differences in culture and worldviews. For instance, individuals may have different perceptions of youth because of their circumstances. In most African nations, the term "youth" usually refers to unmarried individuals aged twenty to forty. In contrast, in Western culture, the phrase may denote individuals in their teenage years, usually between twelve and twenty. This chapter, however, defines "youth" as individuals aged sixteen to thirty. They have social needs and possess the ability to contribute to the advancement of society.

Social Justice

Social justice, like youth, is a difficult concept to define. There seems to be no single all-encompassing definition of social justice. However, any definition of social justice is embedded with the notions of equality, equity, rights, and participation. Any discussion on social justice must take into consideration the role these key elements play in the actualization of social justice. Kay and

Jost define social justice as a state of affairs (either actual or ideal) in which (1) benefits and burdens in society are dispersed under some allocation principle (or set of principles), (2) procedures, norms, and rules that govern political and other forms of decision-making preserve the basic rights, liberties, and entitlements of individuals and groups, and (3) human beings, and perhaps other species, are treated with dignity and respect not only by authorities but also by other relevant social actors, including fellow citizens.[3] Hence, the role of young people in the pursuit of social justice remains very significant.

Biblical foundations of social justice

Theologically, the Bible makes it clear that social justice is a mandate for all believers. It is one of the fundamental expressions of our call to discipleship. The good news of the kingdom of God has vital implications for the pursuit of social justice across all generations. Believers' involvement in the quest for social justice is an expression of our faith and a clear reflection of God's kingdom here on earth.

Any discussion about the biblical and theological foundation of social justice must begin with the understanding of justice from God's perspective. God hates injustice and is committed to restoring justice to those who are oppressed (Exod 2:23; Ps 103:6). Justice is also central to the character of God (Deut 17–18; Ps 45:21). God delights in doing justice, not just because it needs to be done but because that is part of his nature. Similarly, God connects true worship to justice. In Isaiah, God reminds the people of Israel that doing justice is essential to genuine worship and that their prayers, sacrifices, and festivals are abhorrent to him if they fail to act justly. Instead, he calls them to "stop doing wrong. Learn to do right; seek justice. Defend the oppressed. Take up the cause of the fatherless; plead the case of the widow" (Isa 1:10–17). God also connects doing justice to knowing him (Jer 26:11–19).

Several biblical passages outline the need for believers to pursue social justice. We read in Micah 6:8, "And what does the LORD require of you? To act justly and to love mercy and to walk humbly with your God?" In the Bible, the word justice usually emphasizes action, urging believers to treat people equally. Biblical justice means that people get what they deserve as image bearers of our God. Hence, we must treat people equally without reference to their social, political, or economic class. Psalm 146:7–9 gives us a clear picture of the kind of justice that is demanded by the God whom believers serve:

---

3. Kay and Jost, *Social Justice*, 1122.

> [The LORD] upholds the cause of the oppressed
>   and gives food to the hungry.
> The LORD sets prisoners free,
>   the LORD gives sight to the blind,
> the LORD lifts up those who are bowed down,
>   the LORD loves the righteous.
> The LORD watches over the foreigner
>   and sustains the fatherless and the widow,
> but he frustrates the ways of the wicked.
> (see also Lev 19:15; Deut 15:7–11; 16:20; Prov 21:15; Isa 1:17;
>   61:8; Hos 12:6; Amos 5:24; Zech 7:9; Luke 4:18–19)

God requires that, as believers, we be fair to others and act towards all with dignity and reverence, not only in the church but in our homes, schools, workplaces, and communities at large. We must also be aware that standing for justice and fighting for justice comes with consequences. We may face opposition from all angles, but we must be aware that God calls us to act justly as part of our Christian spirituality. However, we can be encouraged by the fact that God's compassion and justice always go together. When we face opposition in our fight for justice, God will stretch out his arm and help us.

Burks argues that "as Christians, social justice takes on a new meaning – a meaning grounded in divine love."[4] This divine foundation sanctions us as believers to pursue social justice in a way that the rest of the world cannot. He added that our pursuit of social justice is "anchored in the commandments God has given, social justice becomes an activity ordained by Christ."[5]

The Role of Youth in Social Justice

Historically, young people have come together on different occasions to form a united force and become a voice in decisions that affect their lives. For example, the civil right movements in America enjoyed the involvement of children and youth. According to the Library of Congress, "At its height in the 1960s, the Civil Rights Movement drew children, teenagers, and young adults into a

---

4. Josh Burks, "Social Justice and Theology," *George Fox University Bruin Blog*, https://www.georgefox.edu/bruin-blog/posts/2021/02/social-justice/index.html#:~:text=Anchored%20in%20the%20commandments%20God,sense%20of%20urgency%20and%20authority.

5. Burks.

maelstrom of meetings, marches, violence, and in some cases, imprisonment."[6] They joined the struggle not only to shape their own futures but also to create a more just world for the future generations. Today, young people continue to take to the streets, demanding change in the face of the continued erosion of human rights and rising unemployment.

Youth's primary role in social justice is to serve as agents of change. It is important to note that social justice involves social actors, regardless of age and gender, who have a sense of their agency and social responsibility towards others and society. This implies that when young people recognize or develop their social responsibility, they can identify social structures and systems that tend to suppress the rights of others or treat them unjustly. Once young people begin working to change these oppressive systems, they automatically become subjects, rather than objects, in the social justice movement.[7]

As subjects or agents of change, these youth can be involved in social praxis. Freire defines praxis as "the reflection and actions upon the world in order to transform it."[8] By engaging in social praxis, young people can work to transform society by developing a critical consciousness that will spur them to take social action. Ginwright and Cammarota add that through their praxis, young people can explore their own experiences with oppression and privilege.[9] Moreover, critical consciousness and social action provide them with the tools to understand and change the underlying causes of social processes that perpetuate the problems that tend to evolve into social injustice. In other words, young people can engage with social systems of injustice and become agents of change by utilizing their critical consciousness to drive social action.

More specifically, young people can be involved in social justice in various ways, including but not limited to the ways described below.

First, young people can raise public awareness about issues of social justice. Young people engage in a great deal of networking in both physical and virtual spaces. They can use such networks to promote social justice by harnessing the power of social media to create positive public awareness on issues of injustice. Networking provides resourceful ways to stay organized and focused on causes that are important in the fight against social justice. Creating awareness

---

6. Library of Congress, "Youth in the Civil Rights Movement," in *Civil Rights History Project*, https://www.loc.gov/collections/civil-rights-history-project/articles-and-essays/youth-in-the-civil-rights-movement/.

7. Ginwright and Cammarota, "New Terrain," 82–85.

8. Freire, *Pedagogy of the Oppressed*, 33.

9. Ginwright and Cammarota, "New Terrain," 88.

may take various forms, such as joining groups, posting articles, and sharing individual experiences. Such activities support and encourage community building, awareness, and collaboration.

Second, young people should be encouraged to be active in public participation. Many cultures in Africa do not provide young people with such opportunities, especially because of their age. However, current trends point to the need for change. If the fight for social justice is to be effective, we can no longer ignore the role played by young people. They are a resourceful and dynamic force who, throughout history, have participated, contributed, and even been catalysts in bringing about important and revolutionary changes in various sectors. Their public participation will give them a greater opportunity to be involved in decision-making and to contribute to the fight for social justice.

Third, young people's right to be heard must be supported at all levels. Given cultural practices that exclude young people from decision-making, communities must change their stance and recognize young people's right to be heard. This right to be heard and to be involved in decision-making must be upheld by all stakeholders.

The Implications for Youth Ministry

Given that young people play a significant role as agents of change by engaging in social praxis, youth ministry has the responsibility to provide young people with platforms that will enable them to engage in social action. This means that youth ministry must change its focus from spirituality alone and also incorporate social issues. By doing so, it can help to reawaken young people's critical consciousness so that they can explore their social structures and systems, identify instances of social oppression, and work towards bringing about transformation.

Conclusion and Recommendations

Social justice is not just an area that young people can engage in but an endeavour in which they play a significant role. Therefore, this chapter offers the following recommendations:

1.   Change our perception of youth. Instead of seeing them as part of society's problems, we must recognize that they are often victims of unjust systems and take steps to address those oppressive and unjust systems.

2. Youth ministries should create platforms that will stir the critical consciousness of young people, enabling them to explore their society and confront the injustices around them.

3. The church should initiate programmes that empower youth to actively engage in social action.

Discussion Questions

1. What is social justice?

2. What significant role do youth play in social justice?

3. Why is it important for youth ministry to create a platform that will enable young people to confront social oppression?

4. What practical programs can the church through youth ministry organize to empower the youth to identify and confront the unjust systems in their society?

Bibliography

Anyon, Jean. *Radical Possibilities: Public Policy, Urban Education, and a New Social Movement.* New York: Routledge, 2014.

Freire, Paolo. *Pedagogy of the Oppressed.* New York: Continuum, 2010.

Ginwright, Shawn, and Julio Cammarota. "New Terrain in Youth Development: The Promise of a Social Justice Approach." *Social Justice* 29, no. 4 (2002): 82–95.

Ginwright, Shawn, Julio Cammarota, and P. Noguera. "Youth, Social Justice, and Communities: Towards a Theory of Youth Policy." *Social Justice* 32, no. 3 (2005): 24–40.

Hiebert, Dennis. "The Recurring Christian Debate about Social Justice: A Critical Theoretical Overview." *Journal of Sociology and Christianity* 12, no. 1 (2022): 49–76.

Jost, J. T. and A. C. Kay. "Social Justice: History, Theory, and Research," in *Handbook of Social Psychology*, 5th ed., edited by Susan T. Fiske, Daniel T. Gilbert, and Gardner Lindzey, 1122–65. Hoboken: John Wiley & Sons, Inc., 2010.

Kelly, Paul G. "A Theology of Youth." *Journal for Baptist Theology and Ministry* 13, no. 1 (2016): 3–19.

Contributors

Nathan H. Chiroma is a practical theologian, ordained minister, educator, and academic. He has been involved in ministry and teaching across Africa, in Nigeria, Burundi, Kenya, Zambia, and South Africa. He has a PhD in practical theology from Stellenbosch University, South Africa, and he currently serves as principal of Africa College of Theology, Rwanda.

Ogidi Joshua Dickson is a researcher with academic curiosity and experience in youth work and family discourse with a passion for theological discernment, self-identity formation, healthy family, social and traditional media. He has a PhD in practical theology and missiology from Stellenbosch University, South Africa. He also pastors a church, ECWA Central Area, Abuja, Nigeria.

Cavens Kithinji is a Kenyan scholar and development practitioner with extensive experience in project planning, monitoring and evaluation, and community development across Eastern Africa. He holds a PhD in project planning and management from the University of Nairobi, Kenya, and currently coordinates the Consortium for Advanced Research Training in Africa (CARTA) program at the African Population and Health Research Center (APHRC). Dr. Kithinji has led curriculum development and institutional capacity building in universities and conducted numerous evaluations for international NGOs. His work focusses on youth empowerment, leadership, and evidence-based development. He is passionate about people-driven change and building resilient communities through inclusive and participatory approaches.

Barnabé Anzuruni Msabah is a Congolese theologian, former refugee, and development practitioner. He currently serves as the Theology and Network Engagement Regional Coordinator for Tearfund in East, Central, and Southern Africa. Prior to this, he led Tearfund's Church and Community Transformation work across East and Central Africa. He holds a PhD in practical theology with a specialization in community development from Stellenbosch University, South Africa, where he is also a research associate. Barnabé is the author of *The Wayfarer* (Langham Global Library, 2021), a book that explores forced migration and community development through a faith-based perspective.

Kevin Muriithi Ndereba holds a PhD in practical theology from the University of South Africa. He is presently a lecturer and head of the Department of

Practical Theology at St. Paul's University, Kenya. He is a research fellow at Stellenbosch University, South Africa, and also a research fellow for the Psychology Cross-Training Program for Theologians, University of Birmingham, UK, where he is conducting Templeton research on mental health and youth in Kenyan congregations. He is editor of *Apologetics in Africa* (HippoBooks, 2024) and author of the forthcoming *Youth Ministry after the Pandemic: A Practical Theology from the Global South* (Wipf and Stock, 2025). Kevin is an ordained elder in the Presbyterian Church of East Africa, where he has been involved in ministry for several years.

Shantelle Weber has a PhD in practical theology from the University of Stellenbosch, South Africa, where she is currently an associate professor in the Department of Practical Theology and Missiology. Her research interests are at the intersections of youth ministry, work, and development; faith formation of children and youth, cultural and interreligious studies, and social justice and youth in South Africa; religious education in schools and theological institutions and teaching and learning practices as related to higher education policy. Shantelle is the founding director of Uzwelo Youth Development, where she lives out her passion for training and connecting youth workers with a passion for youth on the continent.

Obed L. Yusuf is the Youth Development Program coordinator and a faculty member in the Children and Youth Ministry Department, Pan Africa Christian University, Kenya. He holds a bachelors in theology from Jos ECWA Theological Seminary, Nigeria, and a masters in children and youth ministry from Pan Africa Christian University, Kenya.

www.ingramcontent.com/pod-product-compliance
Lightning Source LLC
Chambersburg PA
CBHW060358090426
42734CB00011B/2174